Java Programming for Beginners
Learn Programming without Previous Knowledge

Daniel Lorig

October 26, 2016

Instance = creation of an object

Contents

1 Basics of the Language — 5
   1.1 The Compiler and Developing Environment — 6
   1.2 Installation of Java and Eclipse — 6

2 Core Components of the Java Programming Language — 8
   2.1 Making our Java Example Executable — 10
      2.1.1 Creating and Executing Programs in Eclipse — 11
   2.2 Exercises — 12

3 Control Flow: Conditions and Loops — 13
   3.1 Conditions — 13
   3.2 Loops — 14

4 Object Orientation: A Brief Overview — 17
   4.1 Methods — 18
   4.2 Class Definition — 18
   4.3 Usage of Classes/Objects — 21

5 Primitive Data Types — 24
   5.1 Overview — 24
      5.1.1 Truth Values — 24
      5.1.2 Integer Values — 24
      5.1.3 Floating-Point Numbers — 25
      5.1.4 Characters — 26
   5.2 Creating Variables — 26
   5.3 Typecasting — 27
   5.4 Wrapper Classes — 28

6 Expressions and Operators — 30
   6.1 Assignment Operator — 30
   6.2 Arithmetic Operators — 30
   6.3 Division by Zero — 31
   6.4 Unary Operators — 31
   6.5 Comparison Operators — 31
   6.6 Logical Operators — 32
   6.7 Combining Assignment with Operation — 33
   6.8 Increment and Decrement — 34
   6.9 The Conditional Operator ?: — 35
   6.10 Nested Expressions — 36

7 Arrays — 38
   7.1 Accessing the Items — 39
   7.2 Size of an Array — 39
   7.3 Multidimensional Arrays — 39

8 Strings — 41
8.1 Methods and Operations of Strings — 42
8.2 Converting between Strings and Primitive Data Types — 44

9 Classes and Objects — 45
9.1 Characteristics of Classes — 45
9.1.1 Name of the Class — 45
9.1.2 Attributes — 45
9.1.3 Methods — 46
9.1.4 public and private — 46
9.1.5 Getters and Setters — 46
9.1.6 Static Attributes and Methods — 47
9.1.7 Constructors — 48
9.1.8 Parameters and Return Values — 48
9.2 Defining a Class — 48
9.3 Using Classes and Objects — 50
9.3.1 Creating an Instance — 50
9.3.2 Using an Instance of a Class — 50
9.4 Packages — 52
9.4.1 Accessing Classes within Packages — 53
9.5 Enumerations — 54

10 References, Parameters, and Null — 55
10.1 References and Method Calls — 57
10.2 Null References — 59
10.3 Comparison between References — 60

11 Inheritance — 62
11.1 Access Modifiers — 63
11.2 Constructors — 64
11.3 The Mother of All Classes — 65
11.4 Hierarchy of Types — 65
11.5 Overriding Methods — 66
11.6 The equals Method — 68
11.7 Abstract Classes — 69
11.8 Abstract Methods — 69
11.9 Multiple Inheritance — 70
11.10 Interfaces — 71

12 Exceptions — 73
12.1 Catching Exceptions — 74
12.2 Throwing Exceptions — 77

13 Generics — 79
13.1 Generic Methods — 81
13.2 Restricting Types — 82

14 Collections — 84
- 14.1 Lists 84
- 14.2 Sets 86
- 14.3 Associative Memory 87

15 File Management — 91
- 15.1 The Class RandomAccessFile 91
- 15.2 Streams 92

16 Concurrency — 93
- 16.1 Synchronization 94

17 Network Programming — 99
- 17.1 Sockets 99
  - 17.1.1 Port Forwarding 101
- 17.2 Server 101
- 17.3 Client 103
- 17.4 Access to Internet Resources 104

18 Graphical User Interfaces (GUIs) — 106
- 18.1 A Minimalistic GUI 106
- 18.2 GUI Elements 107
- 18.3 Event Handling 111

19 Additional Web Resources — 113
- 19.1 List of Web Resources 113

20 Example Code Downloads — 120
- 20.1 Download 120
- 20.2 Import 120
- 20.3 Exercises 121

21 Imprint — 121

1 Basics of the Language

Java is an object-oriented language that also uses some concepts from imperative programming. Object orientation roughly means that you try to model a program like the real world: you have objects that interact with each other. Imperative programming means that you give a set of instructions to the computer that specify what should be done in which order.

By combining these two paradigms, Java has become one of the most successful and most used languages ever. There are other well-known languages such as C and C++, but Java differs from them because it does not use error-prone concepts such as manual memory management and pointer arithmetic. This makes it easier for beginners to learn the Java programming language.

There's another advantage for beginners who are learning Java: the language is (unlike other programming languages) completely platform-independent. The slogan "Write once, run anywhere" means you can program an application on a Linux system, but the application will run under Windows or Mac too. However, to make this work, Java is missing some system-specific functionalities (e.g., ejection of CD/DVD drive or direct access to the Universal Serial Bus [USB] port).

Another important thing on the way to complete platform independence is the way Java applications are compiled and executed. In languages such as C and C++, you write some code, take this code to a compiler, and the compiler translates your source code to machine code which can finally be executed on your computer. However, there's a limitation: you can execute this machine code only on the platform where the source code was compiled. For example, if you've written C++ code and have compiled it on a Windows compiler, the resulting application can only be executed on Windows machines.

In Java this is different. The source code isn't translated directly into machine code but rather into an "intermediate language" called bytecode. This intermediate language is the same on all platforms (i.e., the bytecode that was generated on a Windows system can be used on a Linux system too). To actually execute the Java bytecode on a computer, you need an interpreter. This interpreter is platform-specific, and this means every platform needs its own interpreter (this is called the virtual machine). Thanks to the widespread use of Java today, there is an interpreter for just about every conceivable platform. This means you actually reach platform independence with Java: you write your code, bring it into an intermediate language with the help of a compiler and then take that bytecode to whatever platform you like; it can be executed then by the existing interpreter for that platform.

The following steps are the standard procedure for programming with the Java language:

1. Write source code in Java

2. Translate the source code into platform-independent bytecode ("intermediate language")

3. Execute the bytecode with the help of an interpreter ("virtual machine")

1.1 The Compiler and Developing Environment

Java is freely available, so it is relatively easy to get the tools that are needed for learning and programming from the Internet. One thing you will definitely need is the Java Development Kit (JDK). It contains important tools such as the compiler, run-time environment, and language documentation. Using this tool kit, you could already start programming and compile and execute your applications from the command line. The JDK is available for download on the Oracle website.[1]

However, it is more convenient to use an integrated development environment (IDE) for programming, especially if you are in the process of learning the language. For Java, there are some very good tools that you can use free of charge. At this point, I want to recommend the Eclipse development environment. You can get it from the official Eclipse website.[2] You can choose "Eclipse IDE for Java Developers" here. Eclipse offers syntax highlighting and some other very useful features for programming convenience. For example, while you are writing your code, Eclipse will continuously compile it in the background and will give you a hint (by underlining the faulty code) when you've made a syntax error that will lead to a compiler error.

You can find a short tutorial on how to install the JDK and Eclipse here.[3]

1.2 Installation of Java and Eclipse

First, you should download the development kit from the Oracle website which was cited in the previous section. You'll find different versions there; it is best to select the latest version from the list. There are also different editions for different operating systems (e.g., Mac OS, Linux, Windows 32 bit [x86], Windows 64 bit [x64]), and you should select the correct edition for your operating system. After the download has finished, you can start the installation. The wizard guides you through the steps and there's no need to edit any settings because you can keep the defaults. After a few minutes Java is installed on your computer.

After Java has been installed, you can continue with the download of Eclipse. You can find an installer for your operating system on the download page for Eclipse. When executing the installer, you'll be asked which edition of Eclipse you want to install. You should select "Eclipse IDE for Java Developers." Confirm all further queries and wait until the installation is complete.

Now you can start Eclipse. You will be asked which directory you want to use as "workspace." The workspace is the directory where all of your future projects will be stored. Select an empty folder or keep the default setting.

---

[1] http://www.oracle.com/technetwork/java/javase/downloads/jdk8-downloads-2133151.html
[2] http://www.eclipse.org/downloads/
[3] https://www.ntu.edu.sg/home/ehchua/programming/howto/EclipseJava_HowTo.html

When Eclipse has started, you will see the welcome screen. You can simply close it. Now you see the working space, which you can customize and personalize, by the way.

The main elements of the working space are as follows:

- The "Package Explorer" on the left side. You will find all of your projects here later, and you can select the file you want to edit.

- The source editor is the large empty space in the middle. If you open a source file later you can edit it here.

In the next chapter you'll see how to create and execute a simple application in Eclipse.

2 Core Components of the Java Programming Language

First and foremost, a Java program is a set of instructions that tells the computer what to do. The processor executes these instructions in the order that they are given. After the last instruction has been executed, the Java application terminates.

Many of the instructions aim to change the value of variables. A variable is simply a memory unit that can contain any value, such as a number or a string (i.e., a word or a sentence). For example, a change to a variable could mean that a number is added to another or that a string is appended to another string.

Now, we will look at some of the core components of a Java program by using a simple example.

```java
int summand1 = 5;
int summand2 = 10;
int sum = summand1 + summand2;
System.out.println(sum);
```

Hint: You can't compile and execute these lines because they do not form a complete program. At this point we are only showing the essentials; later we will show you how the complete programs look.

Maybe you can see the purpose of this program already without having any knowledge of the Java programming language: we want to compute the sum of two numbers and print the result on the command line so that the user can see it. The program consists of four instructions; in general, you write one instruction and close the line with a semicolon. That's the case in many programming languages.

The first instruction is what we call the declaration of a variable with simultaneous assignment. A new variable is created, and it is given the name *summand1*. We can choose whatever name we like for our variables; however, there are some limitations. For example, the name has to start with a letter. To make the program understandable, you should always use meaningful names that will allow you to infer the purpose of the variable.

Variables in Java always have a specified type – that is, the type indicates what kind of variable it is. In this case we use the type `int` for the variable *summand1*, whereby `int` stands for integer and means whole number (e.g., 0, 1, 2, and so on). Now, in the variable *summand1* we can save integer values, but not decimal numbers such as 2.5 or 5.34. Other important data types that you encounter often in Java are `double`, `float` (these types store decimal numbers and the two types differ only in accuracy and value range), and `String` for strings.

In our example, we have the declaration of the variable and simultaneous assignment of a value. In general, we can split this – that is, declare a variable and assign it later:

```java
int summand1;
```

```
summand1 = 5;
```

In general, the syntax for the declaration of a variable is as follows:
```
TYPE NAME_OF_VARIABLE;
```

and the syntax for the assignment of a value is:
```
NAME_OF_VARIABLE = <EXPRESSION>;
```

But what does $<EXPRESSION>$ mean at this point? If you do a value assignment, you do not need to give a specific value every time (as we do in the first and second lines in our example). Rather, you can specify a complex expression and the actual value is automatically computed at the time of the assignment. You can see this in the third line of our example:
```
int sum = summand1 + summand2;
```

Again, we create a value of type `int`. We do not use a specific value for the assignment; however, we use the expression `summand1 + summand2`. When the processor reaches this statement during program execution, the expression is evaluated. In this case that means it will determine which value is stored in the variable *summand1*, then it will determine which value is stored in the variable *summand2*, and finally, the sum of these two values is calculated. This sum is then assigned to the newly created variable *sum*. Because the two variables *summand1* and *summand2* hold the values 5 and 10, the variable *sum* resolves to 15.

The fourth line in the example is significantly different from the previous lines because we do not create a variable here; instead, a function is called. Java has a certain "basic functionality" which we can use at any time; in a way this is a library of important functions that are needed often. In this case it is a function that prints something to the command line.

In general, the syntax for a function call (actually the correct wording would be method call) in Java is as follows:
```
NAME_OF_OBJECT.NAME_OF_METHOD(<LIST_OF_PARAMETERS>);
```

We spoke briefly about objects at the beginning of the book when we introduced the term "object orientation." We won't go much further into objects at this point; however, it is important to know that in Java, the function calls are always paired with concrete objects. We take an example from the real world for an illustration of this: our object could be a stove and the stove could have a method, `cook` (methods are functions). When we call this method, we have to pass one parameter, which is the object that we want to cook. Using Java syntax, this would look as follows:
```
myStove.cook(myBreakfastEgg);
```

This call would mean that the method `cook` is called on the object *myStove* with the parameter *myBreakfastEgg*. Or in plain English: My egg is cooked on my stove.

Now, let's go back to the real Java example. In the fourth line we have the following method call:

```
System.out.println(sum);
```

The function call is happening on an object `System.out`. This object belongs to the "basic equipment" of Java, so we don't need to create it – it's just there. The object provides some functionality for outputting information on the command line. One of the methods of this object is the method `println` (this is short for "print line"). The call of this method causes the variable passed to be printed on the command line and the insertion of a line break afterwards. In this case the content of the variable *sum*, which is 15, is printed to the command line.

This is the only visible action that our example program performs, so we just see the result of the summation on the command line. The other actions (the creation of the variables and the calculation of the sum) only take place internally, and we don't see any of it.

2.1 Making our Java Example Executable

To make the example program that we just learned about executable, we need to embed it into a class framework. At this point, we still don't want to explore classes any further; we just need to know that in Java every code needs to be encapsulated within classes. We therefore need a first class to execute our code. In Java every public class is stored in a separate file, whereby the name of the file is determined by the name of the class – namely, `NAMEOFCLASS.java`.

When we complete our example program by adding a class framework with the class name `MyExampleApplication`, we have to put the code for this class into a file that is named `MyExampleApplication.java`. In the following, we will see the complete class framework for our example program (this is the first complete and executable Java program we have in this book):

```java
public class MyExampleApplication
{
        public static void main(String[] args)
        {
                int summand1 = 5;
                int summand2 = 10;
                int sum = summand1 + summand2;
                System.out.println(sum);
        }
}
```

As we indicated before, a class with the name `MyExampleApplication` is created. The only purpose of this class is to provide an execution framework for our program. The class consists of only a single method – namely, the `main` method. The `main` method is called by the Java interpreter when the Java program is executed, so if you want to execute a Java program, it always needs at least one class with a `main` method. The name of the main method always has to be "main." You can ignore the remaining parts of the method definition (i.e., the words "public", "static", "void" and the expression "String[] args"); we will come back to this later. At this point we only need to make our Java code executable, and all we need for this is a class that has the shown structure.

What might be useful at this point is to know the meaning of the curly brackets ({ and }). Curly brackets are used to mark coherent blocks of code, whereby a coherent block begins with an opening bracket and ends with a closing bracket. In the example above, the first opening bracket (in the second row) and the last closing bracket (in the last row) mark the class `MyExampleApplication`. It's the same for the main method: it is encapsulated within a pair of brackets, an opening one and a closing one.

Now you can save these lines of code to a file called `MyExampleApplication.java`. Afterwards, you can compile it with the Java compiler and execute it. If you do this via the command line, it looks like the following:

```
javac MyExampleApplication.java
java MyExampleApplication
```

The command `javac` calls the compiler, and the source code is compiled into the intermediate code, the bytecode. The bytecode is automatically saved to a file with the name `MyExampleApplication.class`. You can finally execute this file with the help of the Java interpreter by typing `java MyExampleApplication` into the command line. Note that you have to leave out the file extension, so you just give the class name as parameter.

Having seen this once, we suggest you use an integrated development environment such as Eclipse for this in the future because it is much more convenient.

2.1.1 Creating and Executing Programs in Eclipse

You can download all programming examples that are part of this tutorial from our website. You can import them directly into Eclipse and execute them afterwards. There's no need for you to type all the examples yourself. You will find the download link as well as a guide on how to import the files in chapter 20.

Additionally we will show you how to create your own project in Eclipse. Choose "File", "New" and "Java Project" from the Eclipse menu. In the opening wizard you enter your project name (e.g., "testproject"). You can keep the default for the remaining settings. Click on "Finish" to create your project.

Now you can see your newly created project in the package explorer. Expand the view and perform a right-click on the folder "src." Choose "New" and "Class." In the wizard you can specify the name of your first class (e.g., **MyExampleApplication**). In the area

"Which method stubs would you like to create?" you select the first option "public static void main(String[] args)." Click on "Finish" afterwards.

As you can see, a class `MyExampleApplication` has been created and it is opened automatically in the source editor window. The main method `main()`, which we discussed in the previous section, already exists. You can expand the main method by a simple output routine, such as follows

```
public static void main(String[] args) {
        System.out.println("Hello, World!");
}
```

Note: You can remove the automatically generated line starting with "// TODO."

So we've created a first, very basic program with Eclipse, and we can execute it directly. In the toolbar of Eclipse (below the menu) you will see an icon with a green circle containing a white arrow pointing to the right. Right next to this icon there's a black arrow pointing downwards. You can open a context menu when clicking on this black arrow. Select "Run As" and then "Java Application" from the context menu. All of the compiling steps will be performed automatically and the program will execute afterwards.

In the lower part of the work area a window "Console" will open. It will show all of the outputs a program makes (i.e., if you use `System.out.println()`). You should see the message **Hello, World!** there now.

2.2 Exercises

Starting with the second chapter, we have created exercises for every topic that is covered in this tutorial. The best way to learn programming is by actually programming something ("Learning by Doing"). The exercises are created in such a way that you need to apply the newly learned concepts directly.

We suggest you try to solve the exercises in every chapter after you finish studying the respective chapter. It might be the case that you can't find solutions for all exercises without help. That's no problem; however, you should really try to find a solution on your own first before looking at the example solutions provided.

You will get access to all exercises in chapter 20. Check it now because it is the right time to start with the exercise for chapter 2.

3 Control Flow: Conditions and Loops

3.1 Conditions

Before we get into the topic of object orientation, we will look at some more indispensable components of the Java programming language. So far, we have seen that we can execute a series of instructions one after the other. But we need more control; for example, we want to have an instruction that will only run sometimes rather than on each program execution. This is achieved by using the "if statement":

```
if (<CONDITION_FULFILLED>)
{
        Instruction 1;
        Instruction 2;
        ...
}
else
{
        Instruction 3;
        Instruction 4;
        ...
}
```

With the "if statement," it is first checked if a certain condition is met (we will look into what forms a condition later). Only upon fulfillment of the initial condition are specific instructions executed (i.e., instructions 1 and 2). On the other side, if the condition is not fulfilled, the instructions that are grouped after the "else keyword" are executed. You can see that we use curly brackets to group the parts of the code that are executed on condition fulfillment and condition failure, respectively.

You can omit the else part completely. In this case, the entire block is simply skipped if the condition is not met.

Also note the deviation from the standard syntax that we introduced at the beginning: there's no semicolon directly after the "if statement," there is only one after every single instruction that forms the body of the statement.

Now we extend our programming example with the sum calculation by an "if statement":

```
int summand1 = 5;
int summand2 = 10;
int sum = summand1 + summand2;
System.out.println(sum);

if (sum > 10)
{
        System.out.println("Sum is larger than 10");
}
```

The change is pretty simple: at the end, the program checks, if the value that is stored in the variable sum is larger than 10. If this is the case, it will simply print an additional message on the command line.

This example also shows how a condition can be formulated. Often the condition is an expression that uses a comparison operator. The comparison operators are $<$, $<=$, $==$, $!=$, $>=$ and $>$ (less than, less than or equal, equal, not equal, greater than or equal, greater). A condition can also be a more complex expression than in the previous example, e.g.,

```
summand1 * 5 >= summand2 / 3
```

which means that the condition is fulfilled if the product of *summand1* and 5 is greater than or equal to the quotient of *summand2* and 3.

3.2 Loops

Conditions will also come in handy when using the next concept we are going to learn. Imagine what you would do if you wanted to execute a single instruction or a set of instructions multiple times. With the knowledge gained so far, we have to write down the instruction(s) as often as we wanted it/them to run. Of course, this is a little bit complicated and seems unnecessary, and indeed it is. Programming languages therefore introduced the concept of loops. There are several different types of loops; here, we will only cover the "for loop" and the "while loop."

Let's start with the "for loop." Its general syntax is as follows:

```
for (<INITIALIZATION>; <CONDITION>; <INCREMENT>)
{
        Instruction 1;
        Instruction 2;
        ...
}
```

This might look a little weird at first glance, but in fact, it's relatively easy. Initialization means you can specify code that's executed once at the very beginning of the loop's execution (actually it's executed before the first execution of the loop body). Usually, this is used to create a counting variable, i.e., a variable that is used to count how many times a loop has passed.

The condition is checked before each of the executions of the loop. This is a condition like the one you already know from the "if statement."; you can use whatever condition you like. As the condition is checked before each pass of the loop, the body is only executed if the condition is fulfilled. If the condition is not met, the loop terminates. Note: this means you can have a loop that never executes the body (if the condition is not met on the very first check), or you can have an infinite loop that runs forever (if the condition is met every time); however, you should usually try to avoid these situations.

Increment means that you can insert code that is executed after every pass of the loop. Usually, you would use this to update the counting variable; in many cases, this is by adding 1 to it ("increment").

Below we see a concrete example of a "for loop":

```
int sum = 0;
for (int i = 1; i <= 10; ++i)
{
        sum = sum + i;
}
```

In the initialization part of the loop, a counting variable i of type `int` is created, and it is assigned the initial value of 1. The condition, which is checked before every pass of the loop body, checks if the counting variable i is still lower than 10. As long as this is the case, the loop body gets executed.

In the increment part of the loop, we see something that we haven't seen before:

`++i`

But what does this mean? Well, it's just an abbreviation of

`i = i+1`

`++i` means the counting variable i is incremented by one. This is a very common task in many programming languages; therefore, the programming languages provide the shown abbreviation. (Actually, this also works with `--i`, which would decrement the variable by 1.)

The body of our loop just adds the value of the counting variable to an initially created summing variable. This means that in the end, we will get the sum of the numbers 1 to 10 (which is 55).

To illustrate, let's go through this in a little more detail.

1. At the beginning, the variable *sum* has a value of 0, which is assigned to the variable upon creation.

2. The loop starts with the initialization part; variable i is created and assigned an initial value of 1.

3. Now, for the first time the condition is checked: i is less than or equal to 10 (because i is 1 at this moment), so the loop body will be executed.

4. The value of i (1) is added to the variable *sum* (0), so the *sum* value is 1 afterwards. The loop body only consists of this single instruction, so the first pass of the loop is already completed.

5. As the first pass is completed, the increment part of the loop will be executed (as it will be after every pass). Because the counting variable i is incremented by one, its value is now 2.

6. Beginning with the second pass, the initialization part won't get executed again, so there's another check of the condition. The variable i (which has a value of 2) is still less than or equal to 10, so the body gets executed a second time.

7. Again, the value of i (2) is added to the variable *sum* (1), which will lead to the variable *sum* having the value 3.

8. The second pass is now finished, and the increment part (which will increment the counting variable i) gets executed again.

9. This continues until i has the value of 10. When that value is reached, the loop body is executed one last time. The variable i will be incremented to 11 afterwards, and the subsequent checking of the condition $i <= 10$ fails. The loop finally terminates.

If you understood this, you won't have problems with the other type of loop, the "while loop." The "while loop" is very similar to the "for loop," but there is no initialization and no increment part. The "while loop" only consists of a condition and a loop body that gets executed as long as the condition is fulfilled. The syntax is the following:

```
while (<CONDITION>)
{
        Instruction 1;
        Instruction 2;
        ...
}
```

The same example we used with the "for loop" can be implemented using a "while loop." All we have to do is move the initialization part to the outside of the loop and add the increment part to the end of the loop body:

```
int sum = 0;
int i = 1;

while (i <= 10)
{
        sum = sum + i;
        ++i;
}
```

4 Object Orientation: A Brief Overview

Object orientation is the most important concept in Java, because it is omnipresent in the programming language. Object orientation means you try to model a program as a set of interacting objects like in the real world. This way you can reduce a program's complexity, because you're looking at each object separately rather than trying to implement the program as a whole.

This is the idea behind it. Now, let's look at how it's implemented in Java. In Java, there are classes, which are groupings of similar objects.

For example, a possible class would be `Human`. Specific objects of the type `Human` could be *Aunt Beatrice* or *Scott Powell*. We say *Aunt Beatrice* and *Scott Powell* are instances of `Human`.

So the important thing at this point is: classes are types that group similar objects. Objects are instances of classes.

The characteristic thing about classes is that all instances of a class (i.e., the objects) have the same properties and can perform the same actions; however, the actual values of the properties can differ from instance to instance.

In our `Human` example, this could mean, for example, that all `Humans` (i.e., instances of the class `Human`) have a height and a weight, but the actual values of these properties differ from human to human. What they all have in common is the set of actions they can perform, e.g., *go*, *run*, or *swim*.

In Java terminology, the properties of classes are called "attributes" and the actions are called "methods." A class essentially consists of attributes and methods. Attributes are implemented as variables like `int` or `String`, ones we already know. An attribute can also be an instance of a class. For example, the class `Human` could have an attribute *Best Friend*, so that the attribute would refer to another instance of `Human`.

Methods are functions, and a function is simply a number of lines of code that you may want to run several times. You group the lines of code you want to run several times into a function. Afterwards, you just need to "call" the function when you want to execute these lines instead of writing down all the lines of code every time you want the code to be executed.

Functions also can have parameters. When we call a function, we can pass variables or objects to it, and these parameters can be used when the function is executed. In addition, a function can have an optional return value; this value (or object) will be given back at the end of the function execution to the place where the function was called originally.

4.1 Methods

That was a lot of theory, so we will start illustrate these ideas with a simple example. We write a function that computes the sum of the first n numbers (i.e., 1 + 2 + 3 + ... + n), where n is changeable. This function is the following:

```
public int calculateSum(int n)
{
        int sum = 0;
        for (int i = 0; i <= n; ++i)
        {
                sum = sum + i;
        }
        return sum;
}
```

Let's start with the syntax: The keyword `public` means the method (as part of a class, as we will see later) is open to the public. We will look into that public idea a little bit later; for the time being, we can ignore it. `int` is the return type, which means that at the end of the function execution, we want to return a value of type `int` to the original calling place in the code. You can write functions that don't return any value at the end too; in this case, you'd give the return type as `void`.

`calculateSum` is the name of the function/method. We will refer to that name if we want to call the method later on. After the name, the list of parameters follows. In this case, we only have a single parameter. An int value is passed, and we can choose whatever name we like (here: *n*); that name is used to refer to that parameter in the function body. When we write a function with multiple parameters in the parameter list, these parameters must be separated by commas.

The function body is the same we already know from the example with the "for loop" from the previous chapter: the sum of the first n values is calculated using the loop. What's new is the return statement at the end; it means we want to return the result of our computation to that point in the code where the function is called. Using this function is very simple now:

```
int sum1 = calculateSum(10);
int sum2 = calculateSum(20);
```

In the end, *sum1* will have the value 55, whereas *sum2* will have the value 210.

4.2 Class Definition

We now know the most important components of a class and want to look at how these things come together to form a real class. We'll stay with the previously discussed class `Human`.

```java
public class Human
{
        private int height;
        private int weight;

        private int position;

        private int energyLeft;

        public Human(int _height, int _weight)
        {
                height = _height;
                weight = _weight;

                position = 0;

                energyLeft = 100;
        }

        public int getHeight()
        {
                return height;
        }

        public int getWeight()
        {
                return weight;
        }

        public int getPosition() {
                return position;
        }

        public void move(int distance)
        {
                if (energyLeft >= distance)
                {
                        position = position + distance;
                        energyLeft =
                            energyLeft - distance;
                }
        }

        public void refreshMe()
        {
                energyLeft = energyLeft + 50;
        }
}
```

Annotations: `private int height/weight/position/energyLeft` — defining an integer (must be numeric value). `public Human(int _height, int _weight)` — constructor (gives class meaningful attributes).

Let's start with the syntax. The definition of a class is really simple, the keyword `public` (which simply means that the class is open to public access) is followed by the keyword `class`, which is followed by the freely selectable name of the class (here: Human). After that, we see a big code block that is encapsulated within a pair of curly brackets; that's the actual class definition.

At the beginning, we create the attributes (i.e., the properties) of the class. The attributes `height` and `weight` should be self-explanatory, but we need to say something about the attributes `position` and `energyLeft`. At a later point in time, we want to create instances from this class, i.e., objects. We want to imagine this like it would be in the real world: every human has a well-defined position at any time (one that could be given by coordinates, for example). In our case, that concept is extremely simplified; we just take an `int` value as the current position of a human (i.e., 0, 1, 2, ...).

With the attribute `energyLeft`, we store a value that indicates how much energy an object of type `Human` still has. This again is extremely simplified, but we want to use this in terms of a human being only able to perform certain actions if he/she has enough energy left. (Analogy to the real world: if you come home late from work tired and exhausted, you probably don't have enough energy to run a marathon.)

The definition of the class features keywords like `private` and `public` again, and we want to get into this now. `private` means an attribute (or a method) can't be accessed from the outside. That's the case for our attributes `height`, `weight`, `position` and `energyLeft`, and it means these attributes can only be accessed within the class definition itself. We can access these attributes when defining other parts of the class `Human`, but these attributes can't be accessed from other parts of our program, i.e., from other classes.

`public` is the opposite: we can access attributes or functions that are marked `public` from the outside, too.

These "access modifiers" are the same for attributes and methods, so `private` methods can be called only within their own class, whereas `public` methods can be accessed from anywhere.

Now let's continue with the definition of the class. After the declaration of the attributes we see the following:

```
public Human(int _height, int _width)
...
```

It looks a little bit like a method/function, but it's a constructor. The constructor is called automatically when an object (i.e., instance of a class) is newly created. Therefore, the constructor is typically used to initialize the attributes of the instance with meaningful values. As is the case with methods, the constructor can be supplied with parameters. The general syntax for the definition of a constructor is the following:

```
public <NAME_OF_CLASS>(<LIST_OF_PARAMETERS>)
{
        Instruction 1;
        Instruction 2;
```

```
        ...
}
```

So in a way, the constructor is defined like a method whose name is the same as the class and for which there is no return type specified. Because of that, it's important that you do not use the return statement within the body of a constructor.

Now let's go back to our specific example. The constructor uses the values that are passed as arguments for initialization of the attributes `height` and `weight`. Furthermore, it sets the `position` value to 0 and the `energyLeft` to 100.

Next, we see some methods, all starting with "get." Such methods are called getters. These are used to give the outside world access to the private attributes. The methods therefore just return the corresponding value so that it can be seen from outside of the class also.

But why are we taking this cumbersome detour? Why don't we give the attributes the `public` modifier at the beginning? Well, in this case that's quite simple. We want to give the outside world read access, but no write access, so values can be read but not changed from the outside. This seems reasonable; why should "the outside" have the ability to change the weight or the height of a human?

The next method in line is `move`. It should perform a single action, namely a movement over a specified distance. It first checks if there is still enough energy left. (For every yard the human wants to move, it needs one energy unit.) If there is not enough energy left at the beginning of the movement, the movement won't be executed and the human remains in his or her initial position. However, if there is enough energy left, the position of the human is amended accordingly, and the energy left is decreased by the distance of the movement. So once the action is complete, the position has changed and the energy left has been reduced.

Because we don't want the human to be stranded somewhere (i.e., he or she can't move because he or she doesn't have any energy left), we need to have some functionality that is able to recharge the energy. In our example, we have a simple method that we call `refreshMe`, it simply increases the energy units by 50.

4.3 Usage of Classes/Objects

Now we have seen how to define a class, but we want to know also how to actually use it. By doing that, we learn another part of the Java programming language: the comments. These are each line in code that starts with a double slash (//); they are simply ignored by the compiler, so they have no influence on the actual execution of the program.

Programmers use comments to add notes and explanations in natural language for difficult parts of the code. While they are not of interest to the compiler, they help other human readers better understand the code.

```java
// Instance auntBeatrice is created
Human auntBeatrice = new Human(160, 55);

// We read the height and the
// value of the new variable beatriceHeight is 160
int beatriceHeight = auntBeatrice.getHeight();

// We read the position and the
// value of the new variable beatricePosition is 0
int beatricePosition = auntBeatrice.getPosition();

// auntBeatrice is moving by 40 yards,
// i.e., her position is 40 afterwards
// and energyLeft is 60
auntBeatrice.move(40);

// beatricePosition now has the value of 40
beatricePosition = auntBeatrice.getPosition();

// There's not enough energyLeft for auntBeatrice
// to move another 70 yards,
// so the movement won't get executed;
// neither position nor energyLeft change
auntBeatrice.move(70);

// beatricePosition still has the value of 40
beatricePosition = auntBeatrice.getPosition();

// auntBeatrice is recharged,
// i.e., energyLeft increases from 60 to 110
auntBeatrice.refreshMe();

// Because there is enough energy now, the movement
// of an additional 70 yards can be executed
// energyLeft reduces from 110 to 40.
auntBeatrice.move(70);

// beatricePosition now has the value 110
beatricePosition = auntBeatrice.getPosition();
```

The program execution should be largely self-explanatory with the explanations given in the comments. But we want to add two notes: at the beginning, we've briefly introduced the syntax for calling a method as

`NAME_OF_OBJECT.NAME_OF_METHOD(<LIST_OF_PARAMETERS>);`

`NAME_OF_OBJECT` is always *auntBeatrice* and the `LIST_OF_PARAMETERS` can be left empty in case a method has no parameters. A constructor call is slightly different (remember: a constructor is used to initialize a newly created object) because it's done with the keyword "new."

So we have the following constructor call:

```
Human auntBeatrice = new Human(160, 55);
```

That call will result in the execution of our defined constructor, whereas the parameters 160 and 55 are passed for the initialization of the attributes. The newly created object is returned automatically (i.e., we don't need a return statement in the constructor) and can be used via its given name *auntBeatrice* in the remainder of the program.

This concludes the introductory Java tutorials. Here we have seen some important concepts of the Java programming language. In the remaining chapters, we will look at further concepts of Java in more detail. We will also give a brief introduction to advanced topics such as network programming, concurrency, and the creation of graphical user interfaces.

5 Primitive Data Types

The previous chapters gave a brief overview of the Java programming language. Now we will look at the most important concepts in a little bit more detail. We will start with the primitive data types.

5.1 Overview

Data Type	Value Range	Example	Description
boolean	true / false	true	logical value (true, false)
char	0 to 65535	A	simple character in Unicode encoding
byte	-128 to 127	12	integer value
short	-32768 to 32767	30000	integer value
int	-2147483648 to 2147483647	-200000	integer value
long	-9223372036854775808 to 9223372036854775807	4147483648	integer value
float	+/-1,4E-45 to +/-3,4E+38	3.8	floating-point number
double	+/-4,9E-324 to +/-1,7E+308	21652430000000000	floating-point number with increased accuracy

There are four groups of primitive data types: truth values (`boolean`), integer values (`byte`, `short`, `int`, `long`), floating-point numbers (`float`, `double`), and characters (`char`).

5.1.1 Truth Values

A `boolean` variable can only record two different values: `true` or `false`. Boolean variables are used if you want to store the result of a condition check.

Example:
boolean b1 = 3 > 2;

In the example, we check whether the number 3 is larger than the number 2. Because this obviously is the case, the newly created variable *b1* will be assigned to the value `true`. We could use that variable in a loop or in an "if statement," for example.

5.1.2 Integer Values

There are various data types of integer values in Java. The different types have different value ranges. This means a variable with a smaller value range consumes less memory than a variable with a larger value range. To design as efficient a program as possible you should try to use the smallest possible data type that covers the required range.

In most cases, you will use `int` variables, as they range from below -2 billion to over 2 billion and therefore cover many cases of application. If needed, much larger ranges can be covered with the `long` data type. When the value range of `long` is insufficient, you can use the Java-integrated class `BigInteger`, which covers even higher value ranges. However, we won't discuss this class here any further.

When choosing an integer data type, we must ensure that we pick a data type that isn't too small. What happens if you try to store a value in a variable that doesn't fit into the data range of the data type? Take a look the following example:

```
byte b1 = 127;
b1 = (byte)(b1 + 1);
```

(Note: When adding two `byte` values, you get an `int` value. To be able to store the result in a `byte` variable, we need an explicit type-cast. We will look at that a little bit later in this chapter. For now we need to know that the type-cast occurs by prepending (byte) to the value to be cast (b1 + 1).)

We create a variable of type `byte`. The value range of byte is only up to 127. We assign the maximum value of 127 to the variable. Now we increase the value by 1. What happens then? What value is stored in the variable *b1* now? Well, if the value range of a data type is exceeded, an "overflow" occurs. This means that after going over the upper limit of the range, it will be flipped over to the lower limit of the range. So the variable *b1* now holds the minimum value of `byte`, which is -128. In most cases, you should try to prevent such overflow by carefully selecting the correct data type.

5.1.3 Floating-Point Numbers

Floating-point numbers are used if you need numbers with decimal places. Floating-point numbers also have a significantly larger value range than do integer numbers. At first glance, it might seem reasonable to use floating-point numbers every time. But floating-point numbers are actually more problematic than integer numbers. With the integer values, we had the problem of overflow when using types with insufficient data ranges. That also applies to floating-point numbers, but they have an additional problem with accuracy.

We have two types of floating-point types in Java: `float` and `double`. But you can't store in them every value that lies within the data range. Floating-point numbers can only take values with a limited accuracy. In concrete terms, this means that digits within a value that lie further to the back will be ignored and become 0.

Example: We have a `float` variable that we initialize with the value 0.1000012345, but its actual value will be 0.10000123. The last two digits can't be saved due to the limited accuracy. The accuracy of a variable of type `double` is much higher than the accuracy of `float` variables, but it's also limited.

Furthermore, there are inaccuracies when calculating with floating-point numbers – even with relatively normal values. For example:

```
double a = 69.82;
double b = 69.2 + 0.62;
```

You probably think the two variables a and b are storing the same value now. But actually, that's not the case. If you output the values of these variables, you see that variable a has the value 69.82, as expected. But for variable b, the value 69.82000000000001 is given. This imprecision is happening because of the way floating-point numbers are stored internally. The details are not of interest for us; we just need to know that floating-point numbers can be inaccurate. If we are doing calculations that require precision, we mustn't rely on the ordinary floating-point numbers of Java but rather use the complex class `BigDecimal` (that is part of Java), which offers more precision. Furthermore, we need to remember that equality checking with floating-point values is dangerous because it can lead to unexpected results. If we had checked the two variables a and b for equality, we would have received `false`, although `true` would be expected. So if you have to check floating-point numbers for equality, you should allow a small tolerance.

5.1.4 Characters

A variable of type `char` can store a Unicode character, such as "a" or "&". A character is specified within a pair of single quotation marks, i.e.

```
char c = 'a';
```

Characters are stored internally as integer values, for example, in the range of 0-255 in accordance with the ASCII code. We will see more of that later in this chapter.

5.2 Creating Variables

As we've seen multiple times, variables are declared like this:

```
NAME_OF_TYPE NAME_OF_VARIABLE;
```

and then a value is assigned to them like this:

```
NAME_OF_VARIABLE = VALUE;
```

We can combine declaration and assignment like this:

```
NAME_OF_TYPE NAME_OF_VARIABLE = VALUE;
```

It's important to know that you mustn't read the value of a variable prior to its first assignment. If you declare a variable but don't assign it a value and try to read it, this would lead to a compiler error.

Example:
```
int i1;
int i2 = i1 + 1;
```

This code will result in a compiler error because you tried to read the value of variable *i1* although there was not an assignment of that variable before.

You can create multiple variables of the same type with a single statement. The general syntax is as follows:
```
NAME_OF_TYPE variable1, variable2, variable3;
```

Here we are creating the three variables – *variable1*, *variable2*, and *variable3* – of type NAME_OF_TYPE. Once again, it is possible to initialize these variables directly with the declaration:
```
int variable1, variable2 = 3, variable3;
```

We create three variables of type `int`, whereby *variable1* and *variable3* won't get initialized, whereas *variable2* receives an initial assignment of value 3.

5.3 Typecasting

You can convert variables of one type to another compatible type. This is called typecasting. You can cast a variable to another type by preceding the variable with the target type within a pair of parentheses. Obviously, you can use this to convert between the various integer types:
```
long long1 = 2000;
int int1 = (int) long1;
```

But this is obvious only as long as the value also fits the new data type. In the example, we converted a `long` value of 2000 to an `int` value of 2000. This isn't a problem because 2000 lies in the data range of the type `int`. But what happens if we cast a value to a smaller type that doesn't contain the value?

Example:
```
int var1 = 300;
byte var2 = (byte) var1;
```

Remember: the data range of byte is only from -128 to 127. When doing such allocation, the previously discussed overflow occurs: int 127 will become byte 127. int 128 will become byte -128 (the minimum value of byte). int 129 will become byte -127, and so on. Therefore, int 300 will become byte 44. In our example, the variable *var2* will contain the byte value 44 at the end.

You can also do type casting between char values and integer numbers. As said before, char values will be stored internally as integer numbers, so you can use the ASCII code to assign a char variable the value "A" like this:

```
char ch = (char) 65;
```

65 is the ASCII code of character "A".

You can also use this to get the ASCII code of a character:

```
int ascii = (int) 'A';
```

The variable *ascii* now has the value 65.

A variable of type char always contains only a single character. Nonprintable characters (like tab or a line break) can be assigned using ASCII code, as shown above. For some very common special characters, there are escape sequences that represent the character directly. The most common escape sequence is "\n," which represents a line break (n stands for "new line").

5.4 Wrapper Classes

Java is object oriented, that is, its programs are designed using objects. Many concepts are based on objects (e.g., you can create a list of objects, as we will see later), and it is problematic that the primitive data types are not objects but instead take a special position. If you can build lists of objects, but primitive data types aren't objects, it means you cannot create lists with primitive data types.

Because of this, there are wrapper classes in Java. An instance of a wrapper class represents a value of a primitive data type. If we had to build such a wrapper class on our own, it would look like this for int:

```
public class Integer
{
        private int intValue;

        public Integer(int myInt)
        {
                intValue = myInt;
        }
```

```java
        public int intValue()
        {
                return intValue;
        }
}
```

In fact, Java already has wrapper classes for all of its primitive data types, which are `Integer`, `Byte`, `Short`, `Double`, `Float`, `Character` and `Boolean`. (You see that in most cases they have the same name as the corresponding primitive data type but are capitalized.) Wrapper classes already have a number of useful methods. For example, you can use them to convert the values of the primitive data types into strings and vice versa.

6 Expressions and Operators

At this point, we already know the basics of data types in Java. You can use the data types to make calculations and operations. In the introductory chapters we have already seen several examples of this like the calculation of a sum of `int` values. But there are more operations in Java you can do with the primitive data types.

6.1 Assignment Operator

We already know the assignment operator. Using "=" assigns a variable to a value. On the left side is the variable that is to be assigned and on the right side is an expression that is to be evaluated.

```
int myInt = 1;
myInt = myInt + 3;
```

In this example, we create the variable *myInt* and initialize it with 1. After that, we do a second assignment and increase the value by 3 so we finally have a value of 4 stored in the variable.

6.2 Arithmetic Operators

Using the arithmetic operators you can do ordinary mathematical calculations. There are the operators + (addition), - (subtraction), * (multiplication), and / (division). There is also the modulus operator % that computes the remainder of an integer division.

Addition, subtraction, and multiplication should be trivial and we won't go into detail with them. You just need to be careful because all of these operations can result in overflows if the range of the data types is exceeded. Furthermore, you can have inaccuracies because of floating-point arithmetic.

The division operator and the modulus operator are worth a closer look. The division operator seems to be trivial too at first glance: it will perform a simple division. But what happens if two integer values are divided and the result actually is a floating-point number?

```
int myInt1 = 5;
int myInt2 = 2;
int result = myInt1 / myInt2;
```

In this case, the integer part of the result is returned. In our example, 5 is divided by 2, which should provide a precise result of 2.5. Because we divided two `int` values, the result also is an `int` value. The decimal part of the result is deleted and the value of 2 is stored in the variable *result*. This would be the same with negative numbers; if we divide -5 by 2, we receive -2 as result.

If we divide an integer value by a floating-point number, the result is automatically converted to a floating-point number. This is also the case if we divide a floating-point number by an integer value: the result will be a floating-point number. This applies in general for all arithmetic operations; as soon as a floating-point number is involved in the operation, the result will be a floating-point number.

```
int myInt1 = 5;
double myDouble1 = 2.0;
double result = myInt1 / myDouble1;
```

In this example, the variable *result* will have the value of 2.5 at the end.

The modulus operator % provides the remainder that arises from an integer division. You may know this from elementary school: 5 divided by 2 gives 2 with a remainder of 1. The programmer says: 5 modulus 2 is 1.

```
int myInt1 = 5;
int myInt2 = 2;
int remainder = myInt1 % myInt2;
```

After the operation the variable *remainder* holds the value of 1.

6.3 Division by Zero

It is well known in mathematics that a division by zero is not defined. So what happens if you perform a division by zero in Java (either with the division operator or with the modulus operator)? Well, in this case an exception is triggered. We will look at exceptions in more detail a little bit later. For now, it suffices to know that a program simply crashes and exits in the case of division by zero. We will see how to prevent that later.

6.4 Unary Operators

The - (minus) operator can be used for subtraction as well as negation of a single expression.

```
int myInt1 = 5;
int myInt2 = -myInt1;
```

The variable *myInt2* holds the value of -5 at the end.

6.5 Comparison Operators

There are a number of operators that can be used for comparison of values of the primitive data types. In particular, these operators are > (greater than), >= (greater than or equal), != (not equal), == (equal), <= (less than or equal), and < (less than).

every operation of one of these operators, the result will be of the type `boolean`, i.e., `true` or `false`. This means you can use a comparison operator directly within an "if statement" or in a loop.

Pay attention to the equality operator: it consists of two equal signs (==). This is to avoid confusion with the assignment operator (=). Note: Assignments are done with a single equal sign, equality checks with a double equal sign.

```
int myInt1 = 5;
int myInt2 = 7;

boolean isEqual = myInt1 == myInt2;
boolean isLower = myInt1 < myInt2;
boolean isGreater = myInt1 > myInt2;
```

Here we can see the usage of these operators: variables *myInt1* and *myInt2* are compared with the help of the equality operator. As there are different values stored in *myInt1* and *myInt2*, the result of the equality check will be `false` and the variable will be assigned to the value `false`.

Because *myInt1* is smaller than *myInt2*, the second expression, `myInt1 < myInt2`, evaluates to `true`.

Variable *isLower* will have the value `true`, whereas *isGreater* will be `false` because *myInt1* is not greater than *myInt2*.

6.6 Logical Operators

Logical operators operate on `boolean` variables. The operators are && (and), || (or), ! (not or negation), and ^ (either / or).

The negation operator is applied to a single `boolean` variable: if *b* holds the value `true`, `!b` is evaluated to `false` and vice versa. The remaining three operators concatenate two `boolean` variables: && evaluates to `true` if and only if both input variables evaluate to `true`. The operator || evaluates to `true` if at least one of the input variables evaluates to `true`. The operator ^ evaluates to `true` if exactly one of the two input variables evaluates to `true` and the other one evaluates to `false`.

The following table shows all evaluations for these three operators:

boolean a	boolean b	a && b	a || b	a ^ b
true	true	true	true	false
true	false	false	true	true
false	true	false	true	true
false	false	false	false	false

Important: it's not only possible to use these operators directly on boolean variables – you can use them on every expression that evaluates to a boolean value too. If we create a function that returns a boolean variable, we can use this function in combination with a logical operator. This leads, however, to a special feature. In some cases it isn't necessary to evaluate every operand of an operator. Consider the following example:

```
boolean myBool1 = false;
boolean result = myBool1 && checkCondition();
```

In the example, the *and* operator works on a variable *myBool1* and a function call of a method `checkCondition()`. The final result of the operator will be true if and only if both operands evaluate to true; it is false otherwise. After the first operand *myBool1* has been evaluated, it is already determined that the overall condition can't be met in any case: *myBool1* is false, thus the overall result must be false, regardless of the result of the function call `checkCondition()`. In this case, evaluation of the overall result is finished after the check of *myBool1*, i.e., the call of function `checkCondition()` won't be executed because the final result has already been determined.

When working with logical operators, you have to keep this in mind. It is particularly important if you have a method that is not only computing a return value, but also has a side effect (for example, in the process of the computation a different object could be changed). You need to remember when using a logical operator that not every operand of the operation must be evaluated.

If necessary, you can force the evaluation of all operands by using the operator & instead of && and by using | instead of ||. When using these replacement operators, all operands are evaluated even if it is not necessary because the final result has already been determined. The & operator always returns the same result as the && operator, and the same applies for | and ||. The only difference is that with the replacement operators, all operands must be evaluated, which can result in different program states due to the side effects of the evaluation of the additional operands.

There's one exception to this rule: of course, it's possible that the program crashes during evaluation of the additional operand. Thus, when using the replacement operators | or & the program would crash, and when using the original operators || or && it wouldn't.

6.7 Combining Assignment with Operation

In Java there is something called "syntactic sugar" used for shortening some very common expressions. For example, you often see the following in Java:

```
myInt = myInt + 8;
```

This means you want to increase a variable by a given amount. This can be abbreviated as

```
myInt += 8;
```

So we combine addition and assignment in a shorter expression. We can do the same with the remaining arithmetic operators:

```
myInt -= 2; // a value of 2 is subtracted from the variable
myInt *= 2; // variable is doubled
myInt /= 2; // variable is divided by 2
myInt %= 2; // variable is assigned the remainder
            // of division by 2
```

You can do the same with logical operators:

```
myBool |= false; // same as:  myBool = myBool | false;
myBool &= true;  // same as:  myBool = myBool & true;
myBool ^= true;  // same as:  myBool = myBool ^ true;
```

6.8 Increment and Decrement

In Java we also have the increment and decrement operators (these operators are responsible for the name of the well-known C++ programming language). Increasing or decreasing a variable by one is a particularly common operation. We call these increment and decrement, respectively. That's what the abbreviations ++ and -- are for:

```
int myInt = 2;
myInt++; // abbreviation for myInt = myInt + 1;
```

In the example shown, *myInt* is initialized with 2 and then incremented, so the final value will be 3. You can also use the increment operator by preceding the variable with it:

```
int myInt = 2;
++myInt;
```

The two examples are equivalent. But why is it possible to both prepend and append the increment and decrement operators? Well, these operators have been created so you can use them along the way. You can increment/decrement a variable while using it in a different expression.

Example:

```
int myInt = 2;
int sum = myInt++ + 5;
```

Here we are calculating the sum of 2 and 5. Furthermore, the variable *myInt* is incremented along the way. The question is, do we calculate the sum first $(2 + 5)$ and then increment the variable (`myInt` = 3) or do we increment the variable first (`myInt` = 3) and then calculate the sum $(3 + 5)$?

This is why it matters if the increment operator precedes or follows the variable. If the operator precedes the variable, the variable is incremented first and then evaluated for calculation of the sum (in our example, the final result would be 8 if the operator would have preceded the variable). But if the operator follows the variable (like it does in our example), we evaluate the variable first for the calculation of the sum and increment it afterwards. In our example, the final result for variable *sum* would be 7.

6.9 The Conditional Operator ?:

We've seen the "if statement" in an earlier chapter. The "if statement" enables a conditional execution of code:

```
int a = 6;
int result;

if (a > 5)
        result = 7;
else
        result = 9;
```

(Note: When we introduced the "if statement", we said the respective code blocks for `if` and `else` are grouped within pairs of curly brackets. If we have a code block that only consists of a single instruction, we can omit the curly brackets. In the example above, this holds for both the `if` block and the `else` block.)

In the example, we check if a variable is greater than 5. On the basis of this, we assign a value of either 7 or 9 to another variable. The conditionally executed code in this case is only a single assignment. We can shorten such constructs using the conditional operator ?:

```
int a = 6;

int result = a > 5 ? 7 : 9;
```

The general syntax of the conditional operator is as follows:

```
CONDITION ? expression1 : expression2
```

At first, the condition is evaluated. In case it evaluates to `true`, `expression1` is evaluated and assigned, otherwise `expression2` is evaluated and assigned.

For our example, this means that it is checked if a > 5. If *a* is greater than 5, the conditional operator returns the first value (7 in the example); otherwise, it returns the second value (9 in the example). The value returned by the conditional operator will be assigned to the variable result. This means that the example with the conditional operator is equivalent to the example with the "if statement."

6.10 Nested Expressions

Until now, we've only seen very simple expressions, mostly performed with a single operation. But, as in mathematics, you can use more complex expressions in the Java programming language.

```
int result1 = 2 * 3 + 5 - 8;
int result2 = result1 > 4 ? 7 * 9 : 2 * 3 - 20;
```

The first expression is still relatively easy; we just see combined arithmetic operations. What you might remember from school also applies here: multiplication and division operators have precedence over addition and subtraction operators. So *result1* will be 3 in the end.

In the second expression we see an application of the conditional operator: it is checked if *result1* is greater than 4. Because this isn't the case, only the expression behind the colon is evaluated: 2 * 3 - 20 will evaluate to -14, so -14 will be the final value for variable *result2*.

But you can combine more of the previously introduced operators, and then it isn't as obvious which operator takes precedence.

Example:

```
boolean a = false, b = false, c = true;
boolean bResult = a && b || c;
```

So what's the final value of *bResult*? Depending on operator precedence, it could be either `true` or `false`:

1) We evaluate `a && b` first. This will be `false`. Thus, the remaining expression will be `false || c`. This evaluates to `true`, because *c* is `true`.

2) We evaluate `b || c` first. This will be `true` (because *c* is true). The remaining expression will be `a && true`. This will evaluate to `false`, because *a* is false.

So the question is what has precedence, the "and" operator && or the "or" operator ||? In fact, "and" is stronger than "or", i.e., the "and" operator has to be evaluated first. For our example, this means that the first scenario from above is correct, *bResult* will finally evaluate to `true`.

The following generally applies: to avoid confusion, you should use parentheses in most cases, i.e., in any case that can't be decided with "multiplication and division over addition and subtraction." There is a long table with all operators that specifies which operators take precedence over others, but in general, you can make your life (and the lives of the people who have to read your code) easier by using parentheses when using such expressions.

If we want to change our example in a way such that the second scenario of the evaluation is correct, we have to use parentheses:

```
boolean a = false, b = false, c = true;
boolean bResult = a && (b || c);
```

7 Arrays

In this chapter, we introduce another special data type: arrays. An array is a collection of objects or values of the same type. If we need five variables of type `int`, we can create five variables manually. But we can use an array also for storing five values. You can think of an array like a list of objects or values.

The declaration of an array looks as follows:

NAME_OF_BASE_TYPE[] NAME_OF_ARRAY;

Compared with the declaration of a normal variable, the declaration of an array features an additional pair of square brackets [ ] after the name of the base type. This command only creates a variable of the array type, but we don't have an actual array at this point. There are different possibilities for the actual creation of the array. We will show this with the help of an example in which we create an array of `int` values in four different ways.

```
// version 1:
int[] array1;
array1 = new int[5];

// version 2:
int[] array2 = new int[5];

// version 3:
int[] array3 = {0, 0, 0, 0, 0};

// version 4:
int[] array4;
array4 = new int[] {0, 0, 0, 0, 0};
```

Both versions 1 and 2 show the default initialization of arrays with the "new" operator. The number inside the square brackets specifies how large the array is, i.e., how many values or objects of the specified type the array can contain. You can't change the size of the array after the initialization. When using the "new" operator, the individual items within the array are initialized automatically. In an `int` array, every item is initialized with 0; the same applies for the remaining integer data types. Arrays of type `boolean` are initialized with `false` values.

Versions 3 and 4 show you how arrays can be initialized with custom values. If you are doing the initialization directly when declaring the array variable (as shown in version 3), it's enough to specify the initialization values in curly brackets. If you want to initialize the array later (as in version 4), you also need the "new" operator. Please note that you don't give the size of the array within the square brackets in this case; it is derived automatically from the number of initialization values.

7.1 Accessing the Items

You can access the items of an array using the operator [ ]. You can both read and write using the operator [ ]:

```
int[] myArray = {1, 3, 5, 7};

int firstValue = myArray[0]; // firstValue is now 1
myArray[0] = myArray[3]; // first position in myArray is 7
firstValue = myArray[0]; // firstValue is now 7
```

The operator [ ] takes the index you want to access. The index is zero based, that is, index 0 is for the first element, index 1 is for the second element, and so on.

If you try to access an index that doesn't exist (i.e., a negative index or an index that's larger than the size of the array), it will lead to an exception that will crash the program.

7.2 Size of an Array

You can read out the size of an array using the attribute "length." This works as follows:

```
int[] myArray = {1, 3, 5, 7};

int myArraySize = myArray.length;
```

The variable *myArraySize* now holds the value of 4.

7.3 Multidimensional Arrays

So far we've only seen one-dimensional arrays. You can think of one-dimensional arrays as lists. But you can create arrays with multiple dimensions. You can think of a two-dimensional array as a table or a matrix:

```
1 7 9 7 2
9 6 1 8 8
2 8 9 2 1
```

How do you create multidimensional arrays and use them? The following example will show you.

```
// version 1
int[][] arrayTwoDim = new int[3][5];
arrayTwoDim[0][0] = 1; // row 0, column 0
arrayTwoDim[0][1] = 7; // row 0, column 1
arrayTwoDim[0][2] = 9; // row 0, column 2
```

```
arrayTwoDim[0][3] = 7; // ...
arrayTwoDim[0][4] = 2;
arrayTwoDim[1][0] = 9;
// ...

// version 2
int[][] arrayTwoDimVersion2 = new int[][]
        {{1, 7, 9, 7, 2}, {9, 6, 1, 8, 8}, {2, 8, 9, 2, 1}};
```

Both versions show how to create the previously shown table as a two-dimensional array. Version 1 creates the two-dimensional array using the "new" operator first, initializing all values with 0. Afterwards, the operator [ ] is used to assign each value individually.

In the second version, the values are initialized directly as desired. Technically speaking, we have an array whose elements are also arrays. And that's the way it is initialized: each row is a single array. The main array consists of three elements (representing the three rows of the table) and these three elements are arrays again, each consisting of five elements (the `int` values of the respective line).

You can also apply this concept to higher-dimensional arrays.

8 Strings

In this chapter we will learn about another important data type in Java: strings. Strings, in some way, have a special position in Java: it's not a primitive data type, but a complex one with methods and properties. But unlike other complex data types, strings can be created and assigned like primitive data types.

But let's start at the very beginning. What is a string? A string is simply a list of `char` values. If you connect char values, you have a string. You can use a string for storing words or phrases. The data type of a string in Java is `String`. Declaration of a string looks the same as the declaration of the primitive data types:

```
String myString;
```

Assignment of strings is similar to the assignment of primitive data types:

```
myString = "Hello world";
```

And, of course, we can combine declaration and assignment:

```
String myString = "Hello world";
```

Strings are always specified within quotation marks. If there's a quotation mark within a string, you have to specify the quotation mark using an escape sequence. If you just use an ordinary quotation mark within a string, the Java compiler thinks it has reached the end of the string. Instead, use quotation marks within strings as follows:

```
String myString = "William says:\"Look, how pretty it is.\" ";
```

The escape sequence \" is used to represent quotation marks: by prepending the backslash the compiler knows this isn't the end of the string, but an actual quotation mark is to be used within the string. There are some other escape sequences that represent nonprintable characters. One of the most used escape sequences is \n, which stands for a line break.

Strings are a complex data type, that is, the instances are objects that have been built using a class. In the introductory chapter about classes, we learned that instances of classes are always created using the "new" operator with a constructor:

```
TYPE_OF_OBJECT myObject = new TYPE_OF_OBJECT(PARAMETER p1);
```

This is where strings have a special position: you can create a string like a primitive data type. Of course, you can create a string using a common constructor call too:

```
String myString = new String("Hello world");
```

8.1 Methods and Operations of Strings

Because it is a complex data type, the class `String` has some methods included for analyzing strings. Strings are immutable, that is, once instantiated they can't be changed. This is not to be confused with the fact that you can assign an entirely new object to a `String` variable:

```
String myString = "How are you?";
myString = "Good, thanks.";
```

In the example, we create a variable *myString* and it is assigned to a new string "How are you?" After that, a new object of type `String` with content "Good, thanks." is created and assigned to the variable *myString*. These are two different objects. After the second object has been assigned to the variable *myString*, the first object "How are you?" still exists, but there's no way to access it anymore. (At first, you could access that object using the variable *myString*, but after *myString* has been assigned to a new `String` object, the connection to the first string is lost.)

In Java (unlike in some other languages, e.g., C++), such a situation is detected automatically, that is, the compiler detects that there is an object that can't be (accessed and) used anymore. The object is to be deleted, and the memory it previously used is to be freed. The only thing we need to know about this is that we don't need to care about the disposal of objects that are not required any longer in Java.

Let's get back to our string. We can call methods of class `String` on our string object. Reminder: method calls have the following syntax:

```
NAME_OF_OBJECT.NAME_OF_METHOD(LIST_OF_PARAMETERS);
```

Let's look on some commonly used string methods. (Please note that this is a partial list of string methods.)

```
String myString = "Hey, you!";
int sizeOfString = myString.length(); // returns number of
                                      // characters within string
boolean isEmpty = myString.isEmpty(); // decides if string is
                                      // empty
boolean isEmptyEquiv = myString.length() == 0;
                                      // same as isEmpty() call
char ch = myString.charAt(5); // returns the sixth character
                              // of the string
boolean cont = myString.contains("hey"); // checks for a
                                         // partial string
int index = myString.indexOf("you"); // checks for position
                                     // of a partial string
boolean equality = myString.equals("hey you"); // compares
                                               // two strings
String conkat = myString + " How are you?";
```

We will now discuss this example in detail. In the second line, we read the length of the string. In this specific case, the length of the string is nine characters, so we receive 9 as result. The next line checks if a string is empty, that is, it has no characters. As the string *myString* in the example is not empty, the call of `isEmpty()` will return `false`. The next line does the same, but in a different way: the `length()` method reads the size of the string and uses the operator `==` for determining whether the length is 0.

Using `charAt()`, you can read a single character within a string. The parameter is used to specify the index of the character we want to read within the string. Whenever you use an index, this starts at 0 in many cases in many programming languages. In our case, this means that you can access the first character of the string using the index 0, the second character using the index 1, and so on. As we are using `charAt(5)` in the example, we will get the sixth character within the string, which is "y." It is important to know that if you try to access an invalid index (i.e., negative or too large), an exception occurs that will crash your program. So if you have a string that consists of ten characters and you try to access the eleventh character (i.e., index 10), your program will crash.

The next line in the example shows the method `contains()`: it checks whether a partial string is contained in an overall string. If that's the case, the method returns `true`, it is `false` otherwise.

But you can do this even more precisely. Using the method `indexOf()`, you can determine not only if a partial string is part of an overall string, but you can also get the position within the original string. The method returns an index indicating the position within the original string. Once again, the index is zero based: index 0 means that the partial string starts directly at the beginning of the original string, index 1 means that the partial string is found starting with the second character within the original string, and so on. In our example, we are looking for the index of "you" within "Hey, you.", which is 5 (the "y" in "you" is the sixth character within the original string, hence the index is 5).

If a partial string is found multiple times within the original string, the position of the first occurrence is returned. If a partial string is not found, -1 is returned.

The next line in the example features the method `equals()`. This method checks whether two strings are the same and returns a corresponding `boolean` value.

Finally, we see how to use the already known operator + with strings. It is used for concatenating two strings; it will return a new string that holds the overall string. The original strings remain unchanged. In our example, this means the string *concat* will be "Hey, you. How are you?" in the end.

You can output strings to the default output (i.e., the console) using `System.out.println()`:

`System.out.println(myString);`

There are many other string methods, but we are not going to discuss them here. For example, there are methods for lexicographical comparison of strings, for extraction of partial strings, for string transformation (e.g., conversion to lowercase letters, removal of empty space), for searching for patterns within strings, for replacing patterns within strings, and for splitting strings.

You can take a look at the official reference of Java if you need; you will find detailed explanations of these methods.[4]

8.2 Converting between Strings and Primitive Data Types

Using the wrapper classes for primitive data types, you can convert numbers (or characters) contained within strings to corresponding data types.

Example:

```
String intAsString = "125";
int intAsInt = Integer.parseInt(intAsString);
```

The wrapper class `Integer` has a static method `parseInt()`. A static method is a method that doesn't need an instance of a class to be called. Reminder: method calls usually need a specific object: `NAME_OF_OBJECT.NAME_OF_METHOD(PARAMETERS)`. This is different with static methods; they don't need an instance and can be called like so: `NAME_OF_TYPE.NAME_OF_METHOD(PARAMETERS)`. We will take a closer look at this a little bit later.

For the moment, we just need to know that we can call the static method `parseInt()` of wrapper class `Integer` to convert the string passed into an `int` value. However, the string may contain arbitrary characters that can't be converted to an integer value. In this case, the call of `parseInt()` would lead to an exception that will crash the program.

You can also take the opposite direction for transforming an integer value into a string. That's what the static method `valueOf()` of class `String` is made for:

```
int intAsInt = 125;
String intAsString = String.valueOf(intAsInt);
```

You can convert back and forth between all other primitive data types and `String` using the same pattern.

---

[4] String Documentation at Oracle.com,
http://docs.oracle.com/javase/7/docs/api/java/lang/String.html

9 Classes and Objects

Java is an object-oriented programming language, and classes play a major role. The object orientation is certainly the heart of Java. In the introductory chapter on object orientation, we have seen a first example of what is a class and what is an object. We didn't go into very much detail there, but we will now.

Remember the basic idea behind the object orientation: a class is a collection of similar objects. The objects are called instances of a class. Human could be a class, and *Hillary* and *Donald* would be instances of this class, i.e., objects. In addition, there could be a class Dog, and *Rocky* would be an instance of the class Dog (but not of the class Human).

So a class groups similar objects. The individual instances, however, can differ in their properties (e.g., with the example of Human, the properties of height, weight, or date of birth can differ between instances).

9.1 Characteristics of Classes

A class is represented by three characteristics: its name, its properties (called attributes), and its methods.

9.1.1 Name of the Class

You should select a name for the class that speaks for itself (e.g., Human but not XG6iks). You can use letters, numbers, and underscores, but no spaces. The name of the class should be unique within the program; there shouldn't be several classes with the same name. However, there is one exception to this rule, which we will see later when discussing "packages."

9.1.2 Attributes

A class can have any number of properties/attributes. An attribute is simply a variable that is assigned to a value of a primitive data type or even to an object (i.e., an instance of a class). You can illustrate this with a simple example: the class Human could have an attribute called weight of type double. Each instance of class Human will have a value for this attribute: for example, instance *Hillary* could have a weight of 140.5, and instance *Donald* could have a weight of 236. In plain English, this would mean Hillary weighs 140.5 pounds, and Donald weighs 236 pounds.

A class is characterized by the fact that every instance of the class has the same properties (attributes), but the actual values of these properties can vary. (All instances of the class Human have a weight, but the actual value differs across instances.)

9.1.3 Methods

Furthermore, a class can have any number of methods. A method is a collection of code instructions that will be executed when the method is called. If you want to execute the same code several times at different places, you can write that code within a method. After that, the method can be called by its name when the code needs to be executed.

Methods are usually bound to the instance of a class: you can't simply call a method on its own but rather in conjunction with a specific instance of a class. Within the body of the method, you can, for example, change attributes of the instance.

Let's imagine this again with the example of the class `Human`. This class could have a method `eatSomething`. The only thing that the method would do is increase the attribute `weight` by 1. This means that if the human eats something, his or her weight increases by one pound. You can use this method only in connection with a concrete instance of the class `Human`, for example with the instance *Donald*. In this case, the variable `weight` of this instance would increase by one. If there are other instances of the class, the attribute `weight` remains unchanged with these instances.

9.1.4 public and private

Both attributes and methods can be `private` or `public`. What does this mean? Well, a private attribute can be accessed from within the class itself only. "Within the class" means "code that is part of the definition of the class, i.e., code that lies within the definition of the methods of the class." This means you can't access a private attribute from another class. The same applies for private methods: you can call them only from within the same class, but not from other classes.

Public attributes and methods, however, can also be used by other classes. The keywords `public` and `private` are called "access modifiers" because they specify from where attributes/methods can be accessed. There are more access modifiers, but public and private are the most important ones. We will see one additional access modifier in a later chapter.

9.1.5 Getters and Setters

You might think the concept of access modifiers seems a little bit awkward first. Why should you limit the access to attributes and methods? This makes the programming unnecessarily complicated, doesn't it?

In object-oriented programming you want to model problems and their solutions with the help of independent objects. An object should be coherent; it should make sense. The object has to have certain interfaces for interacting with the outside world – but the outside world doesn't necessarily need to know the inner parts of the object.

If we have a class Addition and the class has a method addTwoNumbers, it is of importance for the outside world that the class provides a correct solution, but it's not of importance how this solution is computed. There may be different methods for adding two numbers – maybe you even want to use a better, more efficient method in the future. And that is why you don't give access to the inner parts – you can be sure that the inner parts won't be used somewhere else. This enables you to simply remove a private method later or replace it with a more efficient method.

Furthermore we want to ensure that an object is in a consistent state at any point in time. What is a consistent state? Think back to our example class Human with the attribute weight. If the attribute were public, it might simply be changed from outside with any value, including negative values. A person with a negative weight: does that make sense? No, of course not. Therefore, you will make the attribute private and only give access via specific access methods. In these access methods, you can intercept invalid values and make sure that there won't be an assignment with an invalid value from the outside.

With the access methods, there's a distinction between the getters and setters. Getters are used to read the value of a variable, and setters are used to apply changes to the variable. You can intercept invalid values when implementing a setter method. You always have to decide for yourself whether you use getters/setters and what special features they need. You have full control over how your object's data can be accessed.

9.1.6 Static Attributes and Methods

We've seen previously that attributes and methods always refer to a specific instance of a class. But you can create attributes and methods that aren't bound to a specific object but rather to the entire class. These are called "static attributes" and "static methods".

- A static attribute is an attribute that is bound to a class but not to an object. This means the attribute will only have a single value for the whole class: you can't give different values for different instances of the class. It also means that the static attribute can be used when there is no instance of that class at all. Imagine the class Human has a static attribute maximumWeight. You can assign and access this static attribute before there is an actual instance of Human. Once you have assigned a value, this value applies for all instances (i.e., you cannot set a maximum weight for each individual Human but rather a maximum weight that applies for all instances of Human).

- It is similar to a static method, which relates to a class but not to a specific object. You can use a static class even before an instance of the class exists. A static method has no direct access to the non-static attributes and methods of the class, because non-static attributes and methods are coupled with specific instances of the class. If you pass a specific instance as a parameter when calling a static method, the static method has access to the non-static attributes and methods of this instance.

9.1.7 Constructors

There's another special feature with the methods: for creating objects, there's a special method called the constructor. The constructor is used to initialize the object (i.e., assign meaningful values to the attributes). Whenever an instance of a class is newly created, a constructor is used. A class can have any number of constructors.

9.1.8 Parameters and Return Values

When a method is called, you can pass parameters to the method. Parameters are the same as variables, which are created outside the method and then passed to the method for use within the method body. The number of parameters for a method is unlimited. Parameters can be primitive or complex data types.

You can not only pass parameters to the method from the outside, but you can also return a value or an object to the calling point. However, a method cannot return more than one value/object.

9.2 Defining a Class

Although we have seen the most important concepts in theory, we haven't seen a single line of code. The next thing we're going to do is to discuss an example of how a class is defined. We will define the class `Human`, which we have already used multiple times as an example.

Lines starting with "//" are comments that the Java compiler ignores. We use them to include natural-language explanations in the code.

```java
// Class definition has the general syntax:
// public class NAME_OF_CLASS { DEFINITION_OF_CLASS }
public class Human
{
        // We create a private attribute weight of type double.
        // The attribute is declared like a common variable;
        // however, it is preceded by the access modifier (private
        // in this case).
        private double weight;

        // Static attribute maxWeight relates to all instances.
        // When declaring static attributes, the keyword static is
        // inserted between the access modifier and type.
        // Static variables can be initialized directly like
        // non-static variables.
        private static double maxWeight = 270.0;

        // This is the constructor.
        // Constructors have the following general syntax:
```

```java
        // public NAME_OF_CLASS(LIST_OF_PARAMETERS) { INSTRUCTIONS }
        // LIST_OF PARAMETERS is an enumeration of passed parameters as
        // NAME_OF_TYPE NAME_OF_VARIABLE
        // Multiple parameters are separated by commas.
        public Human(double theWeight)
        {
                // Assignment: the attribute weight is initialized with
                // the value passed to the constructor at the time the
                // object is created.
                weight = theWeight;
        }


        // Method eatSomething:
        // Methods are defined with the general syntax:
        // ACCESS_MODIFIER RETURN_TYPE NAME(LIST_OF_PARAMETERS)
        // { METHOD_BODY }
        // RETURN_TYPE specifies the type of the value/object that is
        // returned upon completion of the method's execution.
        // If nothing is to be returned, the return type "void" is
        // used
        public void eatSomething()
        {
                // Attribute weight is increased by 0.5
                weight += 0.5;
        }


        // This is the getter method for the attribute weight.
        // The return type is double.
        public double getWeight()
        {
                // We simply return the attribute weight.
                // Returning values/objects is always done with the
                // "return" statement.
                return weight;
        }


        // This is the setter method for attribute weight.
        // This method can be used for changing the weight of the
        // instance from the outside.
        public void setWeight(double newWeight)
        {
                // The weight is changed only if the new value passed is
                // greater than 0. If a negative value is passed, the
                // attribute weight remains unchanged.
                // Furthermore, it's checked if the weight does not exceed
                // the maximum weight, which is stored in the static
                // variable maxWeight. Access to static attributes is
                // possible via the general syntax
                // NAME_OF_CLASS.NAME_OF_ATTRIBUTE
                // The two conditions are combined using the operator
                // "AND" && - this means both conditions have to be
                // satisfied.
                if (newWeight > 0 && newWeight <= Human.maxWeight)
```

```
                weight = newWeight;
        }
}
```

9.3 Using Classes and Objects

We've just seen how to create a class. Now, we will discuss how to use a class and its objects.

9.3.1 Creating an Instance

A variable that is intended to store an object can be declared just like a simple variable of a primitive data type:

`Human barack;`

Now we've created a variable in which we intend to store an object, but we have no object. Objects are created with the operator "new":

`barack = `**`new`**` Human(180.0);`

Instantiation is done according to the following syntax: `new NAME_OF_CLASS(PARAMETERS)`

This means the constructor is called and the parameters are passed. (Remember: The constructor is used for initialization of a newly created object. The constructor of our class `Human` assigns the attribute `weight` the value that is passed. In this example, the attribute `weight` of object *barack* would be 180.0 after the initialization.)

9.3.2 Using an Instance of a Class

After the instance of a class is created, you can use the object. More precisely, you can access attributes and methods of the instance. (Remember: You can only access `public` attributes and methods from the outside.)

You can access attributes and methods using the point operator (.). The syntax for accessing an attribute is the following:

`OBJECT.ATTRIBUTE`

The syntax for accessing a method is the following:

`OBJECT.METHOD(LIST_OF_PARAMETERS)`

The list of parameters differs from the one used in the definition of the method. When defining the method, the list of parameters was given as a comma-separated enumeration of pairs (`TYPE NAME`). When calling the method, we must not specify the type. A parameter is simply an expression that evaluates to a value or an object.

Look at the following example interaction with the class `Human`:

```
Human barack = new Human(180.0);
barack.eatSomething();
double newWeight = barack.getWeight();

barack.setWeight(300.0);
newWeight = barack.getWeight();
```

We start by declaring a variable of type `Human` that we instantiate with a newly created `Human` object.

Now we call the method `eatSomething`. This means the attribute `weight` of the instance is changed internally. After that, we read out the weight using the getter method `getWeight`. We receive the value of 180.5, which is stored within the variable `newWeight` afterwards. Next we try to change the weight manually by calling the method `setWeight`, giving 300 as a parameter. But let's recall the implementation of the method: it checks whether the new weight does not exceed a maximum weight. We used a maximum weight of 270.0. As we now try to use a weight that exceeds the maximum value, the weight remains unchanged and the final call of `getWeight` provides the value from before, 180.5.

Note: If you access attributes or methods of a class from within the class itself, you don't need the whole expression `OBJECT.ATTRIBUTE` or `OBJECT.METHOD(LIST_OF_PARAMETERS)`. When defining a class, you can access the attributes and methods directly by `ATTRIBUTE` and `METHOD(LIST_OF_PARAMETERS)`. In such cases, it is clear that you want to access the "own" instance.

To make this more clear, look at the method `eatSomething` of the class `Human`. This method accesses and changes the attribute `weight` of the class `Human`. In the method `eatSomething`, the access on the attribute `weight` refers to the attribute of the "own" instance. For example, if you call that method on the instance *barack*, the `weight` attribute of the instance *barack* is changed.

You can make this more explicit by using the keyword `this`. When used within the definition of a class, the keyword `this` always refers to the own/current instance. You can write `this.ATTRIBUTE` or `this.METHOD(LIST_OF_PARAMETERS)` to clarify that you want to access attributes or methods of the own instance.

9.4 Packages

We previously stated that the name of a class must be unique: you can't have two classes with the same name. That is correct but the question is: what is the name of a class?

We've seen the class `Human`. Trivially, the name of this class is `Human`. But in Java, you can group classes that have some connection hierarchically into packages. This means that a package can have sub-packages.

Our class `Human` could be part of the following hierarchy:

```
myclasses
        creatures
                Human
                Animal
        devices
                Robot
                Tractor
externalclasses
        helpingclasses
                Calculator
                StringFunctions
```

According to the hierarchy, the class `Human` would be part of the package `creatures`. The package `creatures` would be part of the package `myclasses`. The package `myclasses` consists of the sub-packages `creatures` and `devices`, and both sub-packages consist of two classes each.

The package hierarchy is part of the full name of a class. The full name of the class `Human` would be `myclasses.creatures.Human`. We could create another class `Human` within the package `devices`, which would be valid because the full name of this class would be `myclasses.devices.Human`. The only limitation is you can't create another class `Human` within the package `creatures`, because the full name would be equal to the full name of the other `Human` class.

How are packages realized in Java? First of all, the package hierarchy must be implemented exactly at the file level, where packages are understood to be directories and classes are understood to be files with the extension `.java`. We need a directory hierarchy that exactly matches the package hierarchy.

For the example shown above, this would mean the main directory consists of two sub-directories: `myclasses` and `externalclasses`. The folder `myclasses` has two sub-folders: `creatures` and `devices`. Each of these two directories contains two `.java` files with the corresponding class definitions. The names of the .java-files need to match the (simple) class names exactly, i.e., the directory `creatures` needs to have the two files `Human.java` and `Animal.java`.

You need to specify the package hierarchy at the top of each source file:

```
package myclasses.creatures;

public class Human
{
...
}
```

9.4.1 Accessing Classes within Packages

You need to know how to access classes that are part of a package hierarchy. Is it required to always use the full name (for example, if we want to create a variable of the corresponding type)?

Remember the following basic rules that answer this question:

1. If we are defining a class that is within the same package as the class we want to access, the simple name suffices. Looking at our example, we could use the name `Human` for creating a variable of type `Human` when we are defining the class `Animal`, which is in the same package as `Human`. We wouldn't need the full name `myclasses.creatures.Human`.

2. If we are defining a class that is not within the same package as the class we want to access, we need the full name. When we are defining the class `Robot` in our example, we need the full name of `Human` if we want to create a variable of type `Human`.

3. Packages are used regularly in Java. This means you often use classes that don't lie within the package of the current class. This would result in the usage of many (long) full names. But there's a shortcut. We can import a class or a whole package at the beginning of the source file by using the `import` statement. After that, the classes are known and you can use the simple name in the source file.

   In our example, this would look like follows:
   ```
   import myclasses.creatures.Human;
   ```

   Putting this at the beginning of the source file, the class `Human` would be imported. If we want to use the class later on, we can use the simple name.

   We can also import a whole package. Let's import the whole package `myclasses.creatures`, so we can use the simple names for the classes `Human` and `Animal`:
   ```
   import myclasses.creatures.*;
   ```

The star * means we want to import all classes of the package. You have to put the import statements in front of the class definition, i.e., after the introducing package declaration but before the class definition:

```
package myclasses.devices;

import myclasses.creatures.*;

public class Robot
{
        ...
}
```

9.5 Enumerations

In Java, there are enumerations, which are a special form of classes. You can use enumerations if you want to represent classes that consist of an exactly specified number of objects, that is, you can enumerate the objects. An example application for enumerations would be the days of the week:

```
public enum Weekday
{
        Monday, Tuesday, Wednesday, Thursday, Friday, Saturday, Sunday
}

// ... Usage ...
Weekday today = Weekday.Tuesday;

if (today == Weekday.Saturday)
        System.out.println("Weekend, finally!");
```

10 References, Parameters, and Null

In this chapter, we will take a closer look at variables, particularly what they are and what happens when passing them as parameters in function calls.

But let's start at the beginning: a variable is a memory unit that can contain a value. When we create a variable, some space somewhere within the memory is reserved so we can store a value there later. We've already seen that we can create a variable without giving it an initial value, so the variable is uninitialized directly after its creation. If we try to access an uninitialized variable, it results in a compiler error.

In Java, there's the clear distinction between primitive data types and complex objects. A variable of a primitive data type always stores just a value, i.e., the corresponding location within the memory contains the actual value. This is different with complex objects: an object isn't just a value, but a complex entity. (Remember our Human class example.) If you create a class variable (i.e., a variable of a complex type), the corresponding location in memory just contains a reference to the actual object.

In plain terms, this means if you create an object (which is complex), the object is located somewhere in memory. If you assign the object to a variable, it isn't the actual object that is stored in the memory location of the variable, but a reference to the object. You can think of a reference as an address: the variable stores the address of the object within the memory.

But why is this important? As we saw in the previous chapter, you can use class variables relatively intuitively. Java handles all the stuff with references and memory locations automatically, so the programmer doesn't need to care about that. But the devil is in the details, and it is, in fact, of great importance that you understand these relationships. Why? Take a look at the following example:

```java
// Example 1:
int a = 7;
int b = a;
a++;

// Example 2:
Human michelle = new Human(169.0);
Human michelle2 = michelle;
michelle.eatSomething();
```

The two examples are structurally very similar: a variable is created and assigned to a value or a new object. In the second step, a new variable is created and assigned to the content of the first variable. In the last step, the original variable is changed. In the first example, it is done by incrementing variable *a*. In the second example, it is done by calling the method `eatSomething` on the object *michelle*, which leads to a change of weight for michelle.

This leads to the following question: what is the value of b at the end and what is the value of attribute `weight` of *michelle2*?

We will go through this in detail. We create a variable *a*. The variable is assigned to a value of 7, i.e., the value of 7 is stored at the memory location that represents variable *a*. After that, a new variable *b* is created and is assigned to the value of variable *a*. This means that when the memory location of variable *a* is checked it is found to contain the value of 7, which is written to the memory location of variable *b*. We now have two memory locations that contain the value of 7.

Next, the variable *a* is incremented: at the memory location of variable *a*, 7 is replaced by 8. Variable *b* remains unchanged because it is in a different memory location and has nothing to do with the increment operation. So the variable *b* remains at the value of 7.

Let's analyze the second example the same way. We create a class variable *michelle* of type `Human`. Furthermore, an object of type `Human` is created with the "new" operator. The newly created object is somewhere within the memory. The variable *michelle* only contains the address of the new object, not the object itself. (To make this more concrete, let's say the object is at address #AB68 within the memory. This means the variable *michelle* now contains the address #AB68.)

After that, a second variable *michelle2* of type `Human` is created. It is assigned to the content of the variable *michelle*, i.e., the address #AB68. Therefore, the variable *michelle2* also contains the address #AB68. This means we have just one object of type `Human`, but we can access it using two variables. Using the variable *michelle*, we call the method `eatSomething`, resulting in an increase of 0.5 of the attribute `weight` of the object, i.e., the initial weight of 169.0 has increased to 169.5. If we check the weight now using the variable *michelle2* (i.e., `michelle2.getWeight()`) we get the changed weight of 169.5 because we have one object that can be accessed using two variables.

Note the difference between the behavior of primitive data types and objects: variables of primitive data types directly store values. If a variable of a primitive data type is assigned to a different variable, only the current value is copied. Subsequent changes to one of these variables have no influence on the other variable.

With references to objects, this is different: because the variable does not contain the actual object, but just the reference to it, the object is not copied upon assignment to another variable; a new reference is created instead. As a result, you have two variables that can access the same object.

Understood? OK, let's see the next example:

```
// Example 3:
Human michelle = new Human(169.0);
Human michelle2 = michelle;

michelle = new Human(175.0);
double weight = michelle2.getWeight();
```

What will be the final value of weight, which is obtained by calling `michelle2.getWeight()`

at the end? Is it 169.0 or 175.0?

We will look through this step-by-step. First, we create a class variable *michelle* of type `Human`. At the same time, a specific instance is created and stored somewhere in memory (let's say the address is #F3A6) and the address (#F3A6) is stored in the variable *michelle*. After that, another variable *michelle2* of type `Human` is created and the value of *michelle* is copied, resulting in the variable *michelle2* also storing the address #F3A6.

But now, a new object of type `Human` is created suddenly (let's say it's at the memory location #A889) and the variable *michelle* is assigned to the new object's address. This means the address of the first object, #F3A6, is removed and the address #A889 is stored into the variable. The first object is accessible only via the variable *michelle2* now; the second object is accessible via the variable *michelle*.

The variable *michelle2* still stores the address #F3A6 of the first object. We didn't make any change to the variable *michelle2*, but just created a new object and assigned it to the variable *michelle*. The original object is unchanged, which means a call of `michelle2.getWeight()` will return the weight of the first object: 169.0.

10.1 References and Method Calls

Now we take a further step and look at what happens with variables when methods are called. Let's start out with a rule of thumb: when calling a method, the values of the variables passed are copied. This means Java automatically creates new variables that take copies of the original variables' values. This happens both with primitive data types and with references/complex objects. For primitive data types, values are copied directly; for references, new variables are created that store the same address. This way of passing parameters to methods is called "Call-by-Value."

Let's see some examples of this for clarification:

```java
// Example 4:
public void mainMethod1()
{
        int a = 8;
        helpingMethod1(a);
        int b = a;
}

public void helpingMethod1(int parameter)
{
        parameter = parameter + 1;
}

// Example 5
public void mainMethod2()
{
```

```
        Human michelle = new Human(169.0);
        helpingMethod2(michelle);
        double weight = michelle.getWeight();
}

public void helpingMethod2(Human human1)
{
        human1.eatSomething();
}

// Example 6
public void mainMethod3()
{
        Human michelle = new Human(169.0);
        helpingMethod3(michelle);
        double weight = michelle.getWeight();
}

public void helpingMethod3(Human human1)
{
        human1 = new Human(175.0);
}
```

(Note: To keep the example clear, we have limited it to the necessary minimum, omitting the class framework. You would need a class framework to execute the example.)

We see three very structurally similar examples. In every example, we have a main method, and within the body of the main methods, a helping method is called each time.

In example 4 we create an int variable and initialize it with the value of 8. The variable is passed to a method that increments the variable by 1. The question is what is the value of variable *b* at the end of the main method?

Well, when calling helpingMethod1 a new variable *parameter* is generated and the value of variable *a* from the mainMethod1 is copied into the variable *parameter* ("Call-by-Value"). Within the body of helpingMethod1, the new variable *parameter* is incremented by one. Because it is a copy, the increment has no effect on variable *a* in the main method. The new value of 9 of the variable *parameter* within the helping method is discarded immediately at the end of the execution of the helping method. Variable *a* in the main method still stores the value of 8. This means when the new variable *b* is created, the value of *a*, which is 8, is copied into the variable *b*. So *b* will have the final value of 8.

Now let's look at example 5: We create an object (let's say it is stored at the address #CF6A) and the reference/address to it is stored in the variable *michelle*. When calling the method helpingMethod2, a new variable *human1* is created and the value of variable *michelle* from the mainMethod2 is copied into that variable. This means, the variable *human1* also stores the address #CF6A. Within the body of helpingMethod2, the method eatSomething is called on the object that the variable *human1* references. So this is the object that was created at the beginning of `mainMethod2`, the object that is stored at memory location #CF6A. The attribute `weight` of this object is increased by 0.5 by the call of `eatSomething`. After the execution of `helpingMethod2` has finished, we go back to the main method where we read the value of `weight` of *michelle* via a call of the getter method `getWeight`. Because it's the same object that has been changed within `helpingMethod2`, we receive a weight of 169.5.

Example 6 shows a small variation of example 5: within the body of `helpingMethod2`, a new object is created (let's say it is stored at the memory location #54A3) and the address of the newly created object is assigned to the variable *human1*. *human1* previously stored the value of the object that was created in the main method (#CF6A), whose address is now replaced in *human1*. The variable *michelle* in the main method still stores the address of the initial object, because a copy of that value has been made for the execution of the `helpingMethod3`. So the final call of `michelle.getWeight()` in the main method will return the `weight` of the initial object that's stored at memory location #CF6A (169.0) because that object has not changed. Within the body of `helpingMethod3`, a new object was created, however the reference of this object was only assigned to the variable *human1*, not to the variable *michelle*.

From these examples we can draw the following three conclusions:

- If a primitive data type is passed to a method call, any change that is made to the value inside the method body has no influence on the outside value of the variable, i.e., it has no effect on the original variable.

- If an object is passed to a method call, only a copy of the reference is created, but no copy of the object itself: any change that is made to the object within the body of the called method via method calls on the passed object endures even after the execution of the method has finished.

- If an object is passed to a method call and we change the reference but not the object, the original object remains unchanged.

10.2 Null References

Variables that contain references can also contain an empty reference. Empty reference means the variable does not point to an address/object; it's just empty. Such empty reference is realized using the keyword `null`:

```
Human donald = null;
```

This is used, for example, if you want to initialize a reference variable with a default value. But you need to be careful because you can't call any methods or access attributes on a null reference. This is reasonable because when there is no object, there is no method to call and no attribute to access. If you try this, an exception will usually crash the program.

If you are not sure whether a reference variable contains a null reference, you should check this explicitly before accessing methods or attributes:

```
if (donald != null)
        donald.eatSomething();
```

10.3 Comparison between References

We've already seen the comparison operators in one of the previous chapters. The equality operator is particularly interesting for comparing objects. But when are two objects actually equal?

```
Human michelle1 = new Human(169.0);
Human michelle2 = new Human(169.0);

boolean isEqual = michelle1 == michelle2;
```

In the example, we create two instances of Human. In both cases we initialize the weight attribute with 169.0, so the two instances seem to be the same. But when evaluating the comparison `michelle1 == michelle2` we get `false`. We have two instances at two different memory locations; the two instances just happen to have the same value for the single attribute. Because the references are only compared and we have two objects at different memory locations, the result of the comparison is `false`. So it is checked if the objects are actually the same (i.e., only one object), but is is not checked if they are different objects that completely look the same.

```
Human michelle1 = new Human(169.0);
Human michelle2 = michelle1;

boolean isEqual = michelle1 == michelle2;
```

In this second example we will get the value `true` as result of the comparison: there is only object, but we have the two variables *michelle1* and *michelle1* for accessing it. References are equal because the reference to the object is stored in *michelle2* via the assignment `michelle2 = michelle1`.

Still, it would be useful if we had a way to detect objects that have exactly the same properties/attributes but are actually different objects.

Many classes define a special method for such comparison. This means that the check for structural equality cannot be performed automatically with our class; we have to provide a corresponding method ourselves for checking if two instances of a class are equal. Many classes define a method `equals` for comparison of two objects.

Such a method usually works as follows: you have an object *obj1*, you call this method `equals` on this object using the parameter *obj2* (which is a different object). The method `equals` checks *obj1* and *obj2* for structural equality. All the individual attributes of *obj1* are compared to the corresponding attributes of *obj2*. If all the attributes are equal, the method `equals` returns `true` (to indicate the two objects are structurally equal); otherwise, `false` is returned to indicate that there is no equality between the objects.

In chapter 11, we will write an `equals` method for our class `Human`. At the moment we are still missing some of the basics, so we will do this later.

11 Inheritance

This chapter will introduce another very important concept in Java (and in object-oriented programming in general): inheritance.

Inheritance means you are deriving a second class from an initial class, whereby the derived class contains all methods and attributes from the original class but has additional attributes and methods. Inheritance is usually used to model an "is-a" relationship (e.g., a human is a creature, a dog is a pet, a pet is an animal, an animal is a creature, and so on). Using inheritance you can model hierarchies of classes. In this context we speak of superclasses and subclasses: `Creature` is the superclass of `Human`, and `Human` is a subclass of `Creature`.

For a better understanding of inheritance and its importance, we will look at a simple example:

```java
public class Employee
{
        public String name;
        public String address;
        public long socialSecurityNumber;
}

public class Customer
{
        public String name;
        public String address;
        public long customerNumber;
        public long[] invoiceNumbers;
}
```

We see two independent classes; programmatically, they are not related in any way. Such classes could be part of accounting software that helps to keep an overview on business processes, for example. The two classes should model objects from the real world, particularly, employees and customers. In this simple example an employee is characterized by name, address, and social security number, whereas a customer is characterized by name, address, customer number, and an array that contains the invoice numbers of the customer.

It's noticeable that both the customer and the employee classes have the attributes `name` and `address`. This means we can do an "abstraction" at this point: we have two specific classes describing specific objects. We will look for similarities between these classes and build a common superclass for these two specific classes featuring the similarities.

In other words, we have two specific types of objects: employees and customers. We will now try to find a more general term that covers both types of objects. What term would cover both customers and employees? Well, both customers and employees are persons, for example. So a superclass `Person` would be the generalization of the subclasses `Employee` and `Customer`.

Instead of having independent classes `Employee` and `Customer`, we now create a class hierarchy: a superclass `Person` that derives the two subclasses `Employee` and `Customer`.

```java
public class Person
{
        public String name;
        public String address;
}

public class Employee extends Person
{
        public long socialSecurityNumber;
}

public class Customer extends Person
{
        public long customerNumber;
        public long[] invoiceNumbers;
}
```

The example shows how inheritance is implemented in Java: when defining a class, you append the fragment `extends <superclass>` to the name of the class. This results in the newly defined class taking all public attributes and methods from the superclass. So the attributes `name` and `address` from the example are part of the newly created classes `Employee` and `Customer` also. We can use the classes like we would have used them when defining them directly without inheritance (as seen in the introductory example):

```java
Employee employee1 = new Employee();
employee1.name = "Scott Wolf";
employee1.address = "3634 Las Vegas Boulevard, "+
                    "Las Vegas, NV 89109";
employee1.socialSecurityNumber = 123456789012345L;
```

Note: We use the L at the end of the number 123456789012345L to indicate that this is a `long` value. The value is too large for using an `int` variable, so we create a `long` value by appending L. You can use the lowercase letter l also, but because of the possibility of confusion with 1 (one), it is advised to always use the uppercase L.

11.1 Access Modifiers

We said all public methods and attributes will be taken to the subclass. But what about the private attributes and methods? As we already know you can't access private attributes and methods from the outside of the class. Is this the case even when using inheritance?

The answer is yes, this even holds for derived classes; they have no access to private attributes and methods. But let's get back to the access modifiers: we already know `public` and `private`, and we noted earlier that there are more access modifiers. Now we will introduce another access modifier: `protected`. The access modifier `protected` offers the same protection as `private`, with the exception of derived classes: attributes and methods marked as `protected` are in fact accessible within derived classes.

So if we create a class that should act as a base class later on (base class is another term for superclass) and if we want to access the private attributes and methods of the base class from the subclass, we have to use the access modifier `protected` instead of `private`. When deriving a subclass we will have access to the `protected` attributes and methods; when defining another class, we won't have access (as is the case with the `private` access modifier).

11.2 Constructors

Constructors are special forms of methods; however, constructors are not taken over to the subclass when deriving from a base class. By the way, you don't need explicit constructors at all; if you don't implement your own constructor (as is the cases with the classes `Person`, `Employee`, and `Customer` from the previous example), Java will generate a default constructor that initializes all attributes using default values (`null` for reference variables, 0 and `false` for primitive data types).

A constructor that does not have any parameters is called the default constructor. When you implement a constructor for a subclass, the default constructor of the base class is executed automatically at the beginning (i.e., this is implicit, you don't need to write it down). This means that if the base class has an explicit default constructor (i.e., a constructor with no parameters that you have implemented yourself), that constructor is executed when a new object of the subclass is created. This also happens when there is no explicit default constructor in the base class but the default constructor is automatically created by Java.

When defining a subclass, we can explicitly access the constructor of the base class with the keyword `super`. The following code executes the default constructor of the base class:

super();

Please note: This call is needless, as the default constructor is executed automatically if you don't specify it. But you can access other constructors of the base class too (i.e., constructors that take parameters):

super(PARAMETERS);

A class can have any number of constructors; they only need to differ in the list of arguments.

Important: if you want to call a constructor of the base class, you can do so only at the very beginning of the constructor of the subclass. So the constructor call of the base class (via the keyword `super`) has to be the very first line within the body of the subclass's constructor.

You can't access the constructor of the base class from any other method, just from the constructor of the subclass.

11.3 The Mother of All Classes

In fact, all classes in Java are subclasses of the base class `Object`. If you don't specify an explicit base class for your class, Java will automatically and implicitly use the base class `Object`.

The class `Object` has hardly any functionality of its own. It's there so all classes have a common upper class, which can be useful as we will see later. `Object` is thus the "Adam and Eve" of all classes.

11.4 Hierarchy of Types

Inheritance offers more opportunities in connection with classes.

Inheritance models an "is-a" relation. When we have a variable of a specific type, we can assign it to both objects that match the type exactly and objects of a subclass. This means, for example, if we create a variable of type `Object` (the mother of all classes), we can assign any object to it:

```
Object objectEmployee = new Employee();
```

Furthermore, we can create a variable of type `Person` (from our example) and assign objects from both subclasses `Employee` and `Customer`:

```
Person personEmployee = new Employee();
```

Note: if we assign an object of a subclass to a variable of the base class, we only have access to those methods and attributes that are part of the base class. In the last example, we would have access to the attributes `name` and `address` of the object *personEmployee*, but we wouldn't have access to the attribute `socialSecurityNumber` because it isn't part of class `Person` but only of class `Employee`.

However, the attributes and methods of the subclass aren't lost: we can assign the object to a variable of the specific subtype and obtain access to the specific attributes and methods:

```
Person employee = new Employee();
Employee employeeAsEmployee = (Employee) employee;

long socialSecurity = employeeAsEmployee.socialSecurityNumber;
```

To assign a variable of a "lower" type to an object of a superclass, we have to do an explicit type cast. We've seen this already for primitive data types. This works in a similar way here, the type cast is done via the general syntax:

```
(SUBCLASS) OBJECT_OF_BASE_CLASS
```

But we need to pay attention; we can't convert every object of a superclass to an object of a subclass:

```
Person customer = new Customer();
Employee customerAsEmployee = (Employee) customer;
```

You can compile this example, but when it's executed, it will lead to an exception that will crash the program. We have a variable *customer* of type `Person` and this variable stores a reference to an object of type `Customer`. Because the object is of type `Customer` and not `Employee`, the type cast will fail.

Before we perform an explicit type cast, we need to make sure that the object to be converted has the expected type. In Java, there is the `instanceof` operator that you can use to check if an object has the expected type (or subtype).

```
Person customer = new Customer();
Employee customerAsEmployee;
if (customer instanceof Employee)
        customerAsEmployee = (Employee) customer;
else
        customerAsEmployee = null;
```

11.5 Overriding Methods

We've seen previously that public methods are taken over to the subclass when deriving from a base class. But what happens if we implement the same* method within the subclass?

---

*) Let's take a small digression on the topic "same method." When are methods considered to be the same? If they have the same name?

Actually, a class can have multiple methods with the same name. The methods have to differ in their signature, however. The signature of a method is its name in combination with the types of the parameters. If you have two methods with the same name, where the first takes a single `int` parameter and the second one takes a single `string` parameter, this would be OK, for example.

However, methods that have the same name and the same list of parameters but only differ in the type of the return value are not allowed in Java.

So if we are re-implementing a method in a subclass, the method from the base class will be overwritten.

```java
public class A
{
        public int getA()
        {
                return 3;
        }
}

public class B extends A
{
        public int getA()
        {
                return 5;
        }
}

// ...
B b = new B();
int result = b.getA(); // 5
```

When implementing a subclass, you can access the methods and attributes of the base class with the keyword `super` (as long as they aren't marked as `private`):

```java
public class A
{
        public int getA()
        {
                return 3;
        }
}

public class B extends A
{
        public int getA()
        {
                return super.getA() + 2;
        }
}

// ...
B b = new B();
int result = b.getA(); // 5
```

11.6 The equals Method

In the previous chapter, we discussed how comparing reference variables isn't so simple: the variables just contain the addresses/references of the actual objects, so a comparison of such variables will not perform a structural comparison but just a comparison of identity.

The base class `Object` provides a method `equals` for checking two objects for equality. However, the basic version of `equals` just checks for equality of references/addresses (i.e., a == b) also. Because all classes are derived from the superclass `Object`, we can always use the method `equals` instead of the operator `==` when checking for equality between objects.

But if we want to implement a better comparison, we can override the `equals` method in such a way that a check for structural equality is provided. We demonstrate this using the class `Human` from previous chapters:

```java
public class Human
{
        private double weight;

        public double getWeight()
        {
                return weight;
        }

        // ... additional methods ...

        public boolean equals(Object other)
        {
                if (other instanceof Human)
                {
                        Human otherHuman = (Human) other;
                        return otherHuman.getWeight() ==
                                        this.getWeight();
                }
                return false;
        }
}
```

An object of type `Object` is passed to the method `equals` for comparison: you can compare an object to any other object; it doesn't necessarily need to have the same type. Nevertheless, it makes sense that two objects can be structurally equal only if their types match. Therefore, we use the `instanceof` operator first to find out if the comparison object is of type `Human`. If this isn't the case, we can return `false` as the result of the comparison.

If the comparison object has the correct type, we can perform an explicit type cast so we can access the comparison object through a variable of type `Human`. In our simple example, the class `Human` just has a single attribute: `weight`. So we compare the `weight` of the current object (`this`) to the weight of the comparison object (*otherHuman*). If the weights are equal, we consider the objects to be structurally equal; otherwise, we don't consider them to be equal.

In reality, it would make sense to perform a more complex equality check (e.g., check name, address, weight, size, and so on, only considering objects to be structurally equal if all properties match). We just wanted to show the idea behind the `equals` method with a simple example.

11.7 Abstract Classes

We've seen how inheritance can be used for abstraction: we look for similarities between multiple classes and create a common base class using these similarities. The consequence of this is that you can also create instances of the base class.

This may be OK in some cases, but there are cases where it makes no sense to create concrete instances of base classes that are only created for grouping similarities between subclasses. In such cases, you have the possibility to mark a class as `abstract`. You can't create instances from abstract classes (`new AbstractClass()` will lead to a compiler error), but they exist only for being a base class for more specific subclasses.

You can create abstract classes using the keyword `abstract`:

```
public abstract class Person
{
        String name;
        String address;
}

public class Employee extends Person
{
        String socialSecurityNumber;
}
```

In this example, you can't create instances of `Person`, only `Employee`.

11.8 Abstract Methods

Abstract classes can contain abstract methods also (but they don't need to). An abstract method is a method that has no implementation; it just specifies the signature (i.e., name and parameter list) and the return type.

We can't create instances from abstract classes. Therefore, it is possible to specify methods that have no implementation. If a class has an abstract method, any non-abstract subclasses will need to implement that method.

So the idea of the abstract methods is to specify the required functionality of a subclass in the base class. Note: A derived class does not necessarily need to implement all abstract methods of its base class. In this case, the derived class has to also be marked as `abstract`. You can have a non-abstract class only if all abstract methods of the base classes are implemented.

```java
public abstract class Machine
{
        public abstract int calculateEnergyConsumption();
}

public class Robot extends Machine
{
        public int calculateEnergyConsumption()
        {
                int energy = 0;

                // ... additional calculations ...

                return energy;
        }
}

public class PerpetualMotionMachine extends Machine
{
        public int calculateEnergyConsumption()
        {
                return 0;
        }
}
```

The example shows how abstract classes and methods are created: the keyword `abstract` is included in the declaration of the method. Furthermore, there is no implementation for the abstract method; the declaration of the method is simply terminated with a semicolon.

Within the subclasses, the method is implemented normally. When having several subclasses, the implementations can differ. So the perpetual motion machine from our example is not consuming any energy, whereas the robot needs some energy that is computed by the corresponding method.

11.9 Multiple Inheritance

We've seen that we can specify a base class when defining a new class such that the methods and attributes from the base class are taken over to the new class. There are programming languages that allow multiple inheritance, i.e., you can specify multiple base classes for a single class (which means methods and attributes from all base classes are taken over). In Java, however, this is not possible: a class can only have a single direct base class.

Why is this the case? Well, if we have two independent base classes that have the same method (i.e., name and parameter list match), which of these methods is taken over to the subclass? There is no conclusive answer to that question; therefore, there is no multiple inheritance in Java.

11.10 Interfaces

There is the concept of interfaces in Java, which serve as a replacement for multiple inheritance. You can think of an interface as an abstract class that consists only of public, abstract methods.

So you can't create instances from an interface; like an abstract class, an interface is used only to derive concrete subclasses. The interface specifies which methods need to be part of derived classes (we say: a class implements an interface).

A subclass can derive from a single base class; additionally, it can implement any number of interfaces. We don't have the problem of multiple inheritance here: if there are multiple interfaces that contain the same method, this isn't a problem, because there is no implementation in the interface. We need to implement that method in the subclass anyway, so it isn't problematic if the method is contained in multiple interfaces.

Interfaces can't contain constructors: you can't create instances from interfaces and constructors are not inherited; therefore constructors are pointless in interfaces. When declaring interfaces, you don't need to specify access modifiers: all methods are public automatically.

```
interface Buyable
{
        double getPrice();
}

public class Pot implements Buyable
{
        public double getPrice()
        {
                return 10.5;
        }

        public double getCapacity()
        {
                return 6.5;
        }
}

// Usage:
Pot pot = new Pot();
double priceOfPot = pot.getPrice();
double capacityOfPot = pot.getCapacity();
```

```
Buyable potBuyable = new Pot();
double potBuyablePrice = potBuyable.getPrice();
// Attention: You can't access getCapacity() with a
// variable of type Buyable.
```

The example shows declaration and usage of an interface. When defining a class, you specify interfaces that should be implemented via the keyword `implements` followed by the interfaces. If you want to implement multiple interfaces, these are separated by commas:

```
public class Pot implements Buyable, Sellable
```

The specification of implemented interfaces is appended to the specification of a base class (if applicable):

```
public class Pot extends Kitchenware implements Buyable, Sellable
```

We can create variables of interface types. We can assign these variables to objects that implement the interface. As is the case with ordinary base classes with such variables, we have access only to those methods that are part of the interface. If a concrete class has additional methods that aren't part of the implemented interface, we can't access these using the interface variable. We can perform an explicit type cast for accessing all methods of the class.

```
Buyable potBuyable = new Pot();
Pot pot = (Pot) potBuyable;
double capacity = pot.getCapacity();
```

12 Exceptions

We've seen previously that programs can crash if specific errors occur. We call these errors "exceptions" because they occur when a program reaches an "exceptional state," i.e., when there is an event that should not have happened.

There are various situations that can lead to an exception. A very common reason for an exception to occur is if you have a variable that contains a `null` reference, and you are trying to access a method or an attribute with that variable.

```
public class ExceptionTest
{
        private void exceptionTestMethod()
        {
                Human donald = null;

                double weight = donald.getWeight();
        }

        public static void main(String[] argv)
        {
                ExceptionTest test = new ExceptionTest();
                test.exceptionTestMethod();
        }
}
```

If we execute the example, the program crashes and we get the following error message:

```
Exception in thread "main" java.lang.NullPointerException
        at ExceptionTest.exceptionTestMethod(ExceptionTest.java:7)
        at ExceptionTest.main(ExceptionTest.java:13)
```

We are notified that an exception has occurred. The message indicates what type of exception this is: in this case, it is a `NullPointerException`. A `NullPointerException` means you tried to access attributes or methods of a `null` object.

Additionally, the location where the exception occurred is specified. This is done using a "stack trace." In the example, the stack trace consists of the two last rows, both starting with "at." The stack trace contains the calling hierarchy that leads to the exception; the stack trace is read from the bottom to the top.

The execution of the program starts in the method `ExceptionTest.main`. The first instruction creating the variable and the object for `ExceptionTest` is executed correctly. The next instruction contains a call of method `exceptionTestMethod`. This instruction is on line 13 of the program. Because the exception occurs within the execution of this method, the method call is part of the calling hierarchy that leads to the exception and is, therefore, part of the stack trace.

So the first entry of the stack trace (i.e., the entry at the bottom, because stack traces are read from bottom to top) means that on the way to the occurrence of the exception, there was a method call in line 13 of file `ExceptionTest.java` within method `ExceptionTest.main`.

The second entry of the stack trace tells us what happened after that: we are now within the method `ExceptionTest.exceptionTestMethod`. The execution of this method before line 7 of the file `ExceptionTest.java` was OK: The exception that leads to the crash occurred in line 7. In fact we see that there is a call of `getWeight` on the variable *donald*. The variable *donald*, however, was assigned to the `null` reference before, so this could not work.

In Java there are many more exceptions that occur in exceptional situations; you can even define your own exceptions. Some of the most common exceptions that occur regularly with general programming include the `ArrayIndexOutOfBoundsException` (occurs if you try to access a non-existing index of an array) and the `NumberFormatException` (occurs when you try to convert a string to a number with the string not containing a valid number).

12.1 Catching Exceptions

Now we've seen several example situations that can lead to an exception. However, at this point, we don't benefit from this knowledge: the program continues to crash when an exception occurs.

So what's the purpose of exceptions? If an inappropriate parameter is passed to a method, wouldn't it be better to return a status code indicating an error instead of "throwing" an exception? The problem with status codes is that methods usually return results, not status codes. If we return a status code in case of an error (e.g., `null`, -1, 0, or `false`), we have mixed results and status codes. The return statement of the method is used, depending on the outcome, either to return a result or to return a status code indicating an error.

So to avoid the ambiguity of return values, exceptions were introduced into Java. Instead of returning a status code indicating something went wrong, we trigger an exception. However, we will need a means to detect exceptions that occurred and prevent the program from crashing. We want to be able to handle the exceptional situation adequately and allow the program to continue its execution.

In Java, there is the "try-catch" construct to handle this. Within the "try" part you can specify any code that could lead to an exception. If there actually is an exception, you specify code that should handle the situation adequately within the "catch" part of the construct.

So if an exception occurs within the try block, the execution of the try block is stopped and the code in the catch block will be executed. After that the normal execution of the program after the "try-catch" continues. If there is no exception within the try part of the construct, the code in the catch part won't be executed.

We alter the introductory example as follows for catching and handling the exception:

```java
public class ExceptionTest
{
        private void exceptionTestMethod()
        {
                try
                {
                        Human donald = null;

                        double weight = donald.getWeight();
                } catch (NullPointerException e)
                {
                        System.out.println("Attention: Access
                                        to null reference");
                }
        }

        public static void main(String[] argv)
        {
                ExceptionTest test = new ExceptionTest();
                test.exceptionTestMethod();
        }
}
```

The general syntax for the "try-catch" construct is as follows:

```
try
{
        CODE
}
catch (EXCEPTION_TYPE NAME_OF_EXCEPTION_VARIABLE)
{
        CODE FOR HANDLING EXCEPTION
}
```

We put the code that could trigger the exception in the "try" block. The catch clause specifies first what type of exception should be caught. In our example this would be the `NullPointerException`. Exceptions are represented by objects. So if we intercept an exception, we obtain an "exception object" that provides additional information about the exception (e.g., the stack trace). This is why you give a variable name in the head of the catch clause: it will contain a reference to the exception object.

Finally, the body of the catch clause contains the handling for the exception. In our example, we just print an information message that notifies about the access to a null reference. Now the program won't crash at this point; it will continue its execution after the catch clause.

A "try-catch" construct can have multiple catch clauses if we want to intercept multiple types of exceptions.

```java
try
{
        Human donald = null;
        double weight = donald.getWeight();

        String numberAsString = "789p";
        int numberAsNumber = Integer.parseInt(numberAsString);

} catch (NullPointerException e)
{
        System.out.println("Attention: Access to null reference");
}
catch (NumberFormatException nfe)
{
        nfe.printStackTrace();
        System.out.println("Error when converting to int");
}
```

This example also shows how you can use the "exception object": the call of method `printStackTrace()` will print the stack trace like it would if we hadn't intercepted the exception. In this case, the program isn't crashing, but it will only show the calling hierarchy.

By the way, you don't need to catch an exception at the location where the exception occurs. We could change our class `ExceptionTest` as follows:

```java
public class ExceptionTest
{
        private void exceptionTestMethod()
        {
                Human donald = null;

                double weight = donald.getWeight();
        }

        public static void main(String[] argv)
        {
                ExceptionTest test = new ExceptionTest();
                try
                {
                        test.exceptionTestMethod();
                } catch (NullPointerException e)
                {
                        System.out.println("Attention: Access on
                                                null reference");
                }
        }
}
```

The exception occurs within the method `exceptionTestMethod()`, but the "try-catch" construct is part of the main method `main()`. If an exception occurs, it will be pushed up in the method calling hierarchy until a corresponding catch handler is found in a surrounding "try-catch" construct. If there is no exception handler until the top of the stack trace is reached, the exception cannot be handled and the program will crash.

In our example, we moved the exception handler up by one level. It's now within the method `main()`. `main()` is calling the method excceptionTest() where the exception is triggered. If we execute the program now, the result will be the same as before: the exception is caught and the info text is printed. The difference is that if there was another location in code that calls the method `exceptionTestMethod()` but does not perform exception handling, this would cause the program to crash because the exception wouldn't be handled.

We previously said that exceptions are represented by classes. So exceptions are part of a class hierarchy: for a given exception, there could be subclasses and a base class (each representing exceptions again). This is useful if we have several types of exceptions and want to catch them at once (i.e., using a single catch clause). If you specify a base class within the head of a catch clause, exceptions of types of the subclasses are also intercepted. Almost all exceptions are subclasses of the base class `Exception`. If you specify the exception type `Exception` within the head of the catch clause, almost all possible exceptions are intercepted.

12.2 Throwing Exceptions

So far we've only seen exceptions that are automatically generated by Java. These exceptions were triggered by using an inappropriate argument or by trying to access a null reference. But we can throw exceptions ourselves if we want to indicate that an unwanted situation occurred within our own methods.

We could create our own exception class for doing so. Our custom exception class just needs to be derived from the base class of all exceptions, `Exception`. But Java has a large number of exceptions already that we can use ourselves in different situations. Therefore, it's usually not necessary to create our own exception classes.

If we want to indicate there's an inappropriate parameter, we could use the `IllegalArgumentException`, for example:

```java
public class ExceptionTest
{
        private double calculateBodyMassIndex(int heightCentimeters,
                                              double weightKilo)
        {
                if (heightCentimeters <= 0)
                        throw new IllegalArgumentException(
            "heightCentimeters needs to be greater than 0");

                if (weightKilo <= 0)
                        throw new IllegalArgumentException(
            "weightKilo needs to be greater than 0");
```

```java
                double heightMeter = heightCentimeters / 100.0;
                return weightKilo / (heightMeter * heightMeter);
        }

        public static void main(String[] args)
        {
                ExceptionTest test = new ExceptionTest();
                try
                {
                        double bmi = test.calculateBodyMassIndex(190, 0);
                }
                catch (IllegalArgumentException e)
                {
                        System.out.println(e.getMessage());
                }
        }
}
```

The method `calculateBodyMassIndex` calculates the body mass index using the well-known formula weight / height^2 (using metric input values). This calculation makes sense only if both input values are positive: there is no negative (or zero) size and there is no negative (or zero) weight. So the method checks whether these conditions are met. If either of these conditions is not fulfilled, an `IllegalArgumentException` is triggered. This is done using the keyword `throw`. The exception object to be thrown is appended to the `throw` keyword. In our case, we create a new exception object in both cases. The class `IllegalArgumentException` offers the possibility to specify a message when calling its constructor, and that message can contain further information about what exactly went wrong.

We've put the exception handler to the main method where the method `calculateBodyMassIndex` is called. When the exception occurs, the handler gets the exception object that we created in the "throw" statement. With the method `getMessage()`, we can access the message that's stored within the exception object. So the only thing our exception handler does is to print the corresponding message so that the user knows why the calculation failed.

13 Generics

In some situations, you will write a class that has an attribute, and at the time of the creation of the class, you don't know what type the attribute should have. Only later when the class is used do you want to define the actual type of the attribute.

We already know one way to handle this situation: using the type `Object` for the attribute. This is the base class for all objects, i.e., a variable of type `Object` can store all sorts of objects.

```java
public class WithoutGenerics
{
        private Object myObject;

        public WithoutGenerics(Object obj)
        {
                myObject = obj;
        }

        public Object getMyObject()
        {
                return myObject;
        }

        public static void main(String[] args)
        {
                WithoutGenerics wog = new WithoutGenerics("hello");

                String myObject = (String) wog.getMyObject();
        }
}
```

This example class simply saves one object of arbitrary type and provides access to the object using a getter method. Within the `main` method, we store a string using such an object (which is possible because `String` is a subclass of `Object`) and access the string afterwards using the getter method. The getter method provides a general object of type `Object`; therefore we need to perform an explicit type cast to store the object in a variable of type `String`.

So far, so good. This approach has two weaknesses, however. First, you have to do an explicit type cast every time you want to access the object. This is awkward and should be avoided if possible.

As well, it is possible that we might want to store only objects of specific types. Yes, we could have used the specific type directly instead of using the general `Object`, but what if we wanted to have some objects to only store `String` objects, some other objects to only store `Human` objects, and some other objects to only store `Animal` objects? We had to create own classes for every case of application, with all classes having the same logic and only differing in the type of the object it stores. This is awkward too and should be avoided.

To handle these situations nicely, Java offers the concept of generics. This concept is present as the concept of templates in other programming languages. When creating a generic class, you can introduce type parameters into the class. This means at the time you define a generic class, you don't need to specify the exact type for a generic attribute. You need to specify the type only when the class is used, i.e., when an instance of the class is created. Once you have assigned an instance to a specific type parameter, it can't be changed. You can create any number of instances and assign the type parameter for every instance as desired.

Let's see how to implement the introductory example with the help of generics:

```java
public class WithGenerics<T>
{
        private T myObject;

        public WithGenerics(T obj)
        {
                myObject = obj;
        }

        public T getMyObject()
        {
                return myObject;
        }

        public static void main(String[] args)
        {
                WithGenerics<String> wg =
                        new WithGenerics<String>("hello");
                String myObject = wg.getMyObject();

                WithGenerics<Human> wg2 =
                        new WithGenerics<Human>(new Human(169.0));
                Human myHuman = wg2.getMyObject();
        }
}
```

To make a class generic, you simply need to specify the desired type parameter behind the name of the class in arrow brackets. If you want to use multiple type parameters, you separate them with commas.

A type parameter can be any identifier; usually, we use capital letters, starting with T (as in type).

A type parameter introduced at the beginning can be used within the class definition. So in our example, we state that the object we want to store has to be of type T, whereby T has to be specified when an instance is created. Furthermore, we change the type of the parameter of the constructor to be T and adjust the return type of method getMyObject.

Now we are ready to use our generic class. If we want to create a variable, we need to specify how we want to instantiate the type parameter. For the first object, we use the type `WithGenerics<String>`. This means Java is now implicitly generating a type that replaces all occurrences of type parameter T within the class definition with `String`. Furthermore, when creating the instance using the operator "new," we have to provide the assignment of type parameter T. If we use the newly created object and call the method `getMyObject()`, the object that is returned has the correct type `String`.

In our example, we created a second object; here we instantiate the type parameter T with the type `Human`. Therefore, we can store objects of type `Human` within this instance.

So a generic class is like a template for classes. From a single class definition we can create any number of different concrete classes by assigning the type parameters. One restriction applies: only classes can be used as type parameters; primitive data types can't. Because you have wrapper classes for primitive data types, this restriction isn't a big problem.

13.1 Generic Methods

By the way, you don't need to make a whole class generic. You can have individual generic methods within non-generic classes:

```java
public class ClassWithGenericMethod
{
        public <T> T getObject(T object)
        {
                return object;
        }

        public static void main(String[] args)
        {
                ClassWithGenericMethod cl = new ClassWithGenericMethod();
                String s = cl.getObject("hello");
        }
}
```

When you create a generic method, you simply specify the type parameter after the declaration of the access modifier. You can use the type parameter within the method afterwards. Our simple example just returns the object passed directly.

When using the generic method, the compiler automatically detects how the type parameter has been instantiated. We pass an object of type `String` to the method `getObject`, so it's clear the type parameter T has been instantiated with class `String`. There might be cases that don't allow for automatic detection of the type parameter; in these cases we have to specify the type parameter explicitly when using the method:

```java
String s = cl.<String>getObject("hello");
```

13.2 Restricting Types

So far we only used type parameters that can be instantiated with any type. This imposes a restriction for the usage of objects of these types: if we have an object of type T and T could be any type, we know very little about the specific object. Furthermore, this means we can call methods of class `Object` only on this object (because `Object` is the base class of all classes and all classes have inherited the methods from `Object`). We already know the `Object` method `equals`; `toString()` is another one that returns a string representation for any object.

In many situations we want to restrict the usable types for a type parameter so that you can't use every possible type for instantiation of the type parameter. This is possible in Java: we can specify that a type parameter can be instantiated only with a specific type or a subclass of this type.

Recall the class hierarchy from previous examples, `Person` $\rightarrow$ (`Employee`, `Customer`). We can restrict the type parameter so that you can instantiate the parameter only using `Person` or a subclass of `Person`. In this case, we would know an object of this type has the attributes and methods of `Person` at least, so we could access these attributes and methods.

We adjust the example again, so that only the class `Person` or any of its subclasses can be used for instantiation of the type parameter:

```java
public class WithGenerics<T extends Person>
{
        private T myObject;

        public WithGenerics(T obj)
        {
                myObject = obj;
        }

        public String getName()
        {
                return myObject.name;
        }

        public static void main(String[] args)
        {
                Employee bob = new Employee();
                bob.name= "Bob";

                WithGenerics<Employee> wg =
                                new WithGenerics<Employee>(bob);
                String name = wg.getName();

                Customer steven = new Customer();
                steven.name = "Steven";

                WithGenerics<Customer> wg2 =
```

```
                            new WithGenerics<Customer>(steven);
            String name2 = wg2.getName();
        }
}
```

To restrict a type parameter, we add `extends Restrict_Type` to the declaration of the type parameter, where `Restrict_Type` is a real type. When we define the class and encounter variables of the type parameter, we can assume that we have an object of type `Restrict_Type` or of one of its subclasses. So in our example, we can access the attribute name of class `Person` because we restricted the type parameter T to be of type `Person` or a subclass of `Person`.

If we try to instantiate the type parameter with a incompatible type (e.g., `String` in the example), we would receive a compiler error.

14 Collections

We've seen many basic programming concepts of Java in the previous chapters. At this point, we are able to create useful classes and programs on our own.

Fortunately, we don't need to reinvent the wheel with every program we create. Java has a class library that provides many useful predefined classes that you can use in very different situations. The class library provides functionalities for building graphical user interfaces, input and output of data, mathematical functions, network functionality, and collections.

In this chapter, we will look at the concept of collections. If you have an instance of a collection class, you can use the instance for "collecting" several other objects. We already know this from the array concept: we can use an array for storing instances of different classes. But arrays are relatively inflexible: you have to specify the size of the array when creating the array, and it cannot be changed. Furthermore, it's rather cumbersome to find a specific object within an array because we would have to iterate through all elements of the array.

Collections offer solutions by providing classes that are optimized for a variety of purposes. We can divide the collections into lists, sets, associative memories, and queues. We will take a look at the first three types of collections.

14.1 Lists

Lists are similar to arrays. A list can store a sequential arrangement of objects of a specific type. Unlike arrays, the size of a list can change. We can insert and remove objects at any time.

The interface `List` specifies which minimum features a list must have in Java. There are several implementations of the `List` interface in Java (i.e., there are several types of lists). One of the most used implementation is the class `ArrayList`. Let's see how to use that with a simple example:

```java
ArrayList<String> newList = new ArrayList<String>();

newList.add("Hillary");
newList.add("Donald");
newList.add("Barack");

// newList is:
// Hillary, Donald, Barack

newList.add(1, "George");

// newList is now:
// Hillary, George, Donald, Barack
```

```
newList.set(2, "Mickey");

// newList is now:
// Hillary, George, Mickey, Barack

newList.remove(0);

// newList is now:
// George, Mickey, Barack

newList.remove("Mickey");

// newList is now:
// George, Barack

int size = newList.size(); // 2

boolean containsDonald = newList.contains("Donald"); // false

int indexBarack = newList.indexOf("Barack"); // 1

newList.clear(); // newList is empty now

boolean isEmpty = newList.isEmpty(); // true
```

The class `ArrayList` is a generic class. When creating an instance, you can specify the type of the objects you want to store in the list. You can add additional objects to the end of the list by calling the method `add()`. However, you can specify a different position for the insertion of a new object. As you know from arrays, the positions start with 0: if you want to insert an element at the first position, you write `list.add(0, element)`; if you want to insert at the second position, you write `list.add(1, element)`, and so on. Elements that are behind the insertion position will simply be shifted back one position.

Alternatively, you can replace an element at a specific position with a different element. You can do this by using the `set()` method instead of `add()`. Again, you specify an index and the element that was at this position before will be replaced by the new element, so the size of the list won't change in this case.

Finally, you can use the method `remove()` for removing items from the list. As parameter for the method `remove()` you can either specify the zero-based position of the item to be removed or the item itself. Internally, the method `equals()` is used for checking the equality, not the operator `==`. This means if you specify an object to be removed from the list, the list is iterated beginning with the first object, and every object is compared to the object to be removed with the `equals` method. If a match is found, the corresponding object will be removed from the list. Attention: only the first matching object will be removed, so if there are several identical objects in the list, only the first occurrence will be removed.

In addition the class `ArrayList` has some diagnostic methods for retrieving information about the list. You can find out the number of elements in a list with the method `size()`.

You can use the method `contains()` to check if a specified object is included in the list. Using `indexOf()` you can find the position of an object within the list. If you look for the index of an object that's not included in the list, you will get -1 as result.

The method `clear()` removes any elements from the list, and by calling `isEmpty()`, you can check if the list is empty.

14.2 Sets

A main difference between a set and a list is the fact that a set can't contain duplicate items. Each object can be part of a set only once. The interface `Set` defines the minimum functionality for a Java set.

There are several implementations of the `Set` interface. We will take a closer look at one of these implementations, the `TreeSet` class. Objects within a `TreeSet` object are sorted automatically. (For those of you who have a background in computer science: you might have heard of "red black trees," this is what the `TreeSet` is implementing.) So if you insert new elements into the set, it is ensured that the set is still sorted after the insertion procedure is completed. A `TreeSet` is especially useful if you frequently want to search for objects within the set, because the search is implemented very efficiently internally. (For example, in comparison with a list, the search within a `TreeSet` is much faster.)

Now let's look at the usage of `TreeSet`s with a concrete example:

```
TreeSet<String> newSet = new TreeSet<String>();

newSet.add("Hillary");
newSet.add("Donald");
newSet.add("Barack");

// newSet is:
// Barack, Donald, Hillary

String firstElement = newSet.first(); // Barack
String lastElement = newSet.last(); // Hillary

for (String element : newSet)
{
        System.out.println(element);
}

newSet.remove("Donald");

// newSet is now:
// Barack, Hillary

boolean containsDonald = newSet.contains("Donald"); // false
```

```
int size = newSet.size(); // 2

newSet.clear(); // newSet is empty now

boolean isEmpty = newSet.isEmpty(); // true
```

The creation of a `TreeSet` instance is similar to the creation of a list. `TreeSet` is a generic class. Elements can be added using the method `add()`. Unlike with lists, the order of insertion doesn't matter: elements are sorted automatically (in the example, this is simply the lexicographic ordering of strings). With the special methods `first()` and `last()`, you can access the first and the last object of the set, respectively. However, you can't access elements using indices (as you can with lists).

For accessing all elements of a set, you have to iterate through the items using a "for loop." However, the "for loop" is a bit different than the ones we've seen before. The general syntax for this loop is:

```
for (TYPE_OF_ELEMENT ELEMENT_VARIABLE : SET)
{
...
}
```

So for the first pass of the loop, the variable `ELEMENT_VARIABLE` will be assigned to the first element of `SET`. For the second pass, the variable `ELEMENT_VARIABLE` will be assigned to the second element of the `SET`, and so on. In our example, the variable will be assigned to "Barack" for the first pass, "Donald" for the second pass, and "Hillary" for the third pass.

There is also a `remove()` method for removing elements from a set. You can call the method `contains()` for checking if an element is part of a set, like it was with lists. The call of `contains()` is usually much faster when used with `TreeSet`s instead of lists, particularly with very big sets.

The method `size()` returns the number of elements in a set, and `isEmpty()` checks whether the set is empty. By calling `clear()`, you can remove all elements from the set.

Please note that there are different implementations of the `Set` interface within the class library of Java. These implementations have different characteristics (e.g., a set isn't sorted automatically, but insertion order is preserved).

14.3 Associative Memory

The third major group of collections is associative memory, which is also known as mappings. Using mappings, you can map objects to different objects. This is similar to a mathematical function: if you have the function f(x) = 2 * x, the function f is mapping 1 to 2, 3 to 6, 10 to 20, and so on. With Java mappings, you can map any type to any type (with mathematical functions, you usually map numbers to numbers; however, Java mappings enable arbitrary mappings, e.g., numbers to humans, humans to animals, or robots to numbers).

In contrast to mathematical functions, Java mappings are discrete: a Java mapping is a finite function, i.e., there are only a finite number of maps.

==So a mapping element always has exactly two parts: the source element and the target element. The source element is called the "key," and the target element is called the "value."==

==It is important to remember that any key within a mapping is unique, i.e., you can't have different mapping elements with the same key. Values, however, can be used multiple times.==

This is the same as with mathematical functions. In the case of the function $f(x) = 2 * x$, the key 2 is only mapped to the value 4. Each key is mapped to exactly one value, but there can be several different keys that map to the same value (e.g., the mathematical function $f(x) = x^2$ maps both 2 and -2 to 4).

To simplify the representation, we can specify Java mappings as a ordered row of pairs:

(0, "Donald"), (5, "Hillary"), (6, "Barack")

So, in this example, 5 would be mapped to the string "Hillary," 6 would be mapped to the string "Barack," and 0 would be mapped to the string "Donald."

The Java interface `Map` specifies the minimum functionality for a mapping class. There are several different implementations; we will look at the example of the `TreeMap` class. The `TreeMap` is the counterpart to the `TreeSet` from the sets. Elements inserted into the `TreeMap` are sorted by its keys.

Let's start with a simple example illustrating the creation and the usage of a ==TreeMap==:

```java
TreeMap<Integer, String> newMap = new TreeMap<Integer, String>();

newMap.put(5, "Hillary");
newMap.put(6, "Barack");
newMap.put(0, "Donald");

// newMap is:
// (0, "Donald"), (5, "Hillary"), (6, "Barack")

String element = newMap.get(6); // Barack
int firstKey = newMap.firstKey(); // 0

newMap.put(0, "George");

// newMap is now:
// (0, "George"), (5, "Hillary"), (6, "Barack")

newMap.remove(5);
```

```
// newMap is now:
// (0, "George"), (6, "Barack")

for (int key : newMap.keySet()) {
        String value = newMap.get(key);

        System.out.println(key + " is mapped to " + value);
}

boolean containsKey = newMap.containsKey(2); // false
boolean containsValue = newMap.containsValue("Barack"); // true
```

`TreeMap` is a generic class, too. In contrast to lists and sets, we need two type parameters instead of one: the type of the keys and the type of the values. In our example, we chose `Integer` as key type and `String` as value type.

Note: As you already know, you can't use primitive data types as type parameter for a generic class. So instead of `int`, we chose the wrapper class `Integer`. In doing so we see another useful property of Java: "autoboxing." When we need an `Integer` object, we can simply specify an `int` value instead. The Java compiler automatically converts it to an `Integer` object.

When we write the following:

`Integer i = 7;`

the compiler automatically (and implicitly) converts it to be:

`Integer i = new Integer(7);`

In our `TreeMap` example, we have used autoboxing because we always used `int` values as keys. So we add three elements to the `TreeMap`: (5 → "Hillary"), (6 → "Barack"), and (0 → "Donald"). This is done using the method `put()`; the first parameter is the key and the second parameter is the value that the key should be mapping to.

We can access specific mappings with the method `get()`: we pass the key as argument to the method. If a mapping with the specified key is found within the `TreeMap`, the corresponding value is returned. If the key is not found within the `TreeMap`, we will receive the `null` reference as return value of the method call.

The method `firstKey()` returns the first key. The first key is not the key that was inserted first, but the smallest key according to the sorting order.

If we insert an element with a key that's already in the mapping, the previous entry will be overwritten. In our example, the key 0 maps to "Donald" first. Now we insert the value "George" for key 0, so "Donald" will be overwritten and "George" takes its place.

The `TreeMap` class has a function `remove()` too. You pass the key that is to be removed as parameter to the method call.

==We can iterate through the elements of the mapping with a== "for loop." We need the `TreeMap` method `keySet()` to do so. When calling this method on a `TreeMap`, we get a set of all keys of the mapping. We can iterate through this set of keys the same way we already know from the previous section about sets:

```
for (TYPE_OF_KEYS KEY_VARIABLE : MAPOBJECT.keySet())
{
...
}
```

The `KEY_VARIABLE` will be assigned to all keys of the TreeMap when iterating through the keys. By calling the method `get()`, we get the corresponding value, so we can print key and value like we do in the example.

The class `TreeMap` has two "contains" methods: the method `containsKey()` checks whether a specific key is present, and the method `containsValue()` checks whether a specific value is present.

In our example, we don't show the methods `isEmpty()`, `clear()` and `size()`. These methods are part of the `TreeMap` class too. You can use them exactly the same way you use them with lists and sets.

15 File Management

Another important part of many Java programs is the ability to access files. Access means both being able to read and write files.

15.1 The Class RandomAccessFile

The class `RandomAccessFile` provides a very basic possibility for reading and writing files. You pass two parameters to the constructor of the class: the path of the file is the first, and the access mode is the second. Possibilities for the access mode include "r" for reading from a file and "rw" for reading and writing from/to a file.

The file will be opened upon completion of the constructor call, but this only holds if the file exists at the specified location. If the file does not exist, an exception is triggered.

There are several different "read" methods. The default method for reading is `read()`, which simply reads one byte from the file and returns it as an `int` value. The next call of the method returns the next byte, and so on until the end of the file is reached; at that point -1 is returned. There are additional "read" methods for reading `char`, `long`, `double`, or multiple bytes at once from the file.

If a file is opened for writing access, you can use the "write" methods in analogy to the read methods. With the most basic method `write()`, you can write a single byte into the file.

Another important tool is the file position indicator, which specifies the current position within the file. Directly after opening of the file, the file position indicator points to position 0. After the first read or write operation it will point to position 1, and so on. With the help of the method `seek()`, you can jump back and forth within the file and point the file position indicator to any position.

If you are finished processing your file, you should always close the file with the method `close()`.

```
RandomAccessFile newFile =
   new RandomAccessFile("C:\\My Documents\\test.txt", "rw");

newFile.write(65);
newFile.write(69);
newFile.writeDouble(2.5);

newFile.close();

RandomAccessFile oldFile =
   new RandomAccessFile("C:\\My Documents\\test.txt", "r");

int byte1 = oldFile.read(); // 65
```

```
int byte2 = oldFile.read(); // 69
double double1 = oldFile.readDouble(); // 2.5

oldFile.close();
```

Note: When specifying the path of the file, we have used the escape sequence \\ for separating the different folders. The backslash is used for introducing escape sequences in strings (e.g., \n for line breaks), so if we want to include an actual backslash in the string, we have to use the escape sequence \\.

15.2 Streams

File can be accessed also using "streams". The stream concept is built in a way so that you can create more complex streams from simple streams, which enables a very comfortable read or write access to files. Please refer to the web resources in chapter 19 for further information on this topic.

16 Concurrency

So far we've seen purely sequential programs only: programs that start with the first instruction of the main program and work through all instructions one after the other. When the last instruction has been completed, such programs will exit automatically.

In some cases it might be useful, however, to perform multiple tasks simultaneously. This is called "concurrency".

We want to note that traditional computer systems don't allow for real concurrency: there is only one processor and the processor just performs one task after the other. In this case, concurrency is "simulated": the execution switches quickly between the various tasks. So for example, the processor executes instructions from the different tasks alternately, i.e., instruction 1 of task 1, followed by instruction 1 of task 2, followed by instruction 2 of task 1, and so on. Due to the high speed of modern processors, this creates the impression that the tasks are performed simultaneously.

Modern multi core processors allow for real concurrency, but it shouldn't bother us if two tasks are executed simultaneously or quasi-simultaneously.

In computer science, we refer to concurrent tasks within a single program as "threads". Today's computer systems allow for concurrent programs too; we call these processes. In this chapter we will talk about concurrency within a single program, which we call "multi-threading".

Concurrency is important in the context of graphical user interfaces. If you click on a button that starts a complex operation (that takes some time), you don't want the user interface to freeze during the computation. To make this possible, you would perform the timely operation within a separate thread.

Furthermore, if you have operations that use network connections, you want to execute these operations in the background in many cases, because network use introduces waiting times, and you don't want the program to freeze during these times.

The realization of concurrency is relatively simple in Java: there is a class `Thread`. You derive a new class from this base class and override the method `run()`. This method holds the code that should be executed concurrently. For actually executing the code concurrently, you create a new instance of your derived class and call the method `start()`. This leads to the code of method `run()` being executed in the background.

As we know, each class has to be defined within a separate file, and the name of the class must match the file name. If you have many concurrent threads and if you have to create a separate class within a separate file for each thread, this quickly becomes confusing.

Java offers an abbreviation for this purpose. You can derive a class "anonymously" (i.e., you don't need to specify a name) directly at the location where you want to use it. In some way this would be a disposable class: the class is defined, one instance is created directly, and the class is discarded afterwards. This is ideal for the creation of a subclass of Thread for concurrent execution of code.

Let's look at an example:

```java
Thread t = new Thread()
{
        public void run()
        {
                // Time-consuming code that needs to
                // be executed in the background goes here.
        }
};

t.start();

// General code for normal program execution goes here.
```

So we declare a variable *t* of type Thread. new Thread() is used to create a new object. What is new is that it is followed by a code block (encapsulated within curly brackets) that contains the definition of the anonymously derived class. We just override the method run(). We can place any code that we want to be executed within the background into the method run(). After the closing curly bracket of the class definition, we use a semicolon.

So we've created an anonymous subclass of Thread, and we have created an instance of it instantly. We stored the reference to this instance in a variable of type Thread. This is possible because we can store an object of a subclass within a variable of a base class, as we already know.

The concurrent execution of the code in the run() method is started by calling the start() method on the Thread variable. This means the "general code" and the "time-consuming code" are now executed simultaneously or quasi-simultaneously.

16.1 Synchronization

Concurrent programming introduces a new problem that is unknown in purely sequential programming. What happens if two or more threads access the same data simultaneously or quasi-simultaneously?

Well, as long as there is only read access to the data, this isn't a problem. But when you have write operations from different threads on the same data variable, this can lead to severe problems. We will demonstrate this using a very simple example featuring a basic counter. We create a method that just counts how often it is executed. Then we call this method multiple times from different threads:

```java
public class CounterTest
```

```java
{
    private int counter;

    public CounterTest()
    {
        counter = 0;
    }

    public void incrementCount()
    {
        counter = counter + 1;
    }

    public void testCounter()
    {
        for (int i = 0; i < 10; ++i)
        {
            Thread t = new Thread()
            {
                public void run()
                {
                    for (int j = 0; j < 100000; ++j)
                    {
                        incrementCount();
                    }
                    System.out.println(counter);
                }
            };

            t.start();
        }
    }

    public static void main(String[] args)
    {
        CounterTest test = new CounterTest();
        test.testCounter();
    }
}
```

So the class `CounterTest` has a method `incrementCount()` that increments the counting attribute by 1 upon each call of the method. In the method `testCounter()` we create ten threads using a "for loop." Within each of these threads we define a "for loop" again for calling the counting method `incrementCount()` 100,000 times.

So we have ten threads, each of these incrementing the counting attribute 100,000 times: at the end, the counting variable should have the value 1,000,000. To find out the final value of the attribute, we add an instruction for outputting the value of the variable at the end of each thread. So we will get ten outputs (one for each thread), but only the last one is of interest for us, because it specifies the final value of the counting variable.

We execute the program and receive a surprising result:

```
154503
254503
354503
454503
554503
597938
697938
797938
897938
997938
```

If we execute the program again, we receive a different result, but it's still not the one we expected.

```
103975
242998
299991
399991
499991
599991
699991
799991
899991
999991
```

So we will get a different result each time we execute the program. If you execute the example on your computer, you will probably get different results, but in most cases, you won't get the expected result of 1,000,000 in the last line.

Let's recall this: we called the counting method 1,000,000 times, but the counting variable always stores a smaller value at the end and it stores different values when executed multiple times. How is that possible? The problem arises from the simultaneous write access on the variable from different concurrent threads.

We will go through this step-by-step. Imagine the counting variable has the value of 0 at the very beginning. Now we will execute the counting method simultaneously from two different threads. What happens?

The first thread reads the counting variable, the value is 0. But the value will be read simultaneously by the second thread, so it is 0 there too. The first thread increments the variable by 1, thus receiving 1, and 1 is stored within the counting variable. But the second thread has already read the initial value of the variable to be 0, thus also receiving 1 when incrementing the variable. As a result, the second thread will also store the value of 1 in the counting variable.

The two threads have called the counting method already; however, the value of the counting variable is still 1. This is because the two threads have read the value of the variable simultaneously and independently incremented the variable by 1. Because the variable has been read from two threads simultaneously, the same calculation has been carried out within these two threads.

To avoid this problem, we have to make sure that only one thread can access the variable at a time. So if thread 1 reads the variable, thread 2 has to wait until the complete operation (i.e., reading the value, incrementing it, and storing it in the variable) has been completed in thread 1. Thread 2 may read the variable only after the operation in thread 1 is finished.

In Java, you have the possibility to mark "critical sections" within your code that may be accessed by a single thread only at a time. You can imagine this as two railway lines that have an intersection: the intersection is the critical section and only one train can be inside the critical section at a time. If a second train arrives while another train is currently inside the critical section, the second train has to wait until the first train has left the critical section completely.

The same holds for threads in Java: if a critical section is occupied by a thread and another thread wants to enter it, the second thread must wait until the first thread has left. This behavior is called "synchronization".

There are several ways you can realize synchronization in Java; we will show the simplest one here. The easiest way is to simply mark a complete method as a critical section. To do so, you just need to insert the keyword `synchronized` after the access modifier of the method. From now on, only one thread can enter this method at a time (per instance).

So in our example, we simply need to mark the method `incrementCount()` as synchronized:

```java
public synchronized void incrementCount()
{
        counter = counter + 1;
}
```

If we execute the program now, we get the expected result:
```
131172
270333
300000
455224
502285
671307
700000
898221
900000
1000000
```

We can repeat the execution, and we will always get 1,000,000 million as the final value, i.e., the counting variable has been correctly incremented 1 million times.

There are additional possibilities to mark critical sections in Java. These give more detailed control over the synchronization to the programmer. We refer you to the web resources in chapter 19. There, you will also find information about problems that can arise from the usage of critical sections and how to prevent them.

17 Network Programming

In the last twenty years, the Internet hasn't only become very popular – it has become almost an indispensable part of daily life. It's rare that an invention has revolutionized the people's lives so drastically in such a short period of time.

That's the reason why the computer's network connection plays an increasingly important role. If you buy a computer nowadays, you won't get a floppy disk drive; in many cases, you won't even get a CD or DVD drive. However, every computer sold today has a fast network connection and a wireless LAN function.

We often use our computer's network connection in connection with a web browser like Internet Explorer or Mozilla Firefox to view websites. But there are many more applications that use the network connection. Just think of a video game you play online against your friends: data is exchanged using the network connection so that you and your friends can access the same game from multiple machines.

Technically speaking, a network connection is usually established between two endpoints. If you have designed a corresponding program, you can run the program on two different computers and a connection is established between these two computers using the program to exchange data.

Actually, there are many different ways to exchange data between two machines. The two most popular protocols are the "Transmission Control Protocol" (TCP) and the "User Datagram Protocol" (UDP). First, we will introduce the differences between these two protocols.

TCP is similar to a phone call: you enter an address to which you want to connect (phone number) and you establish a connection (phone call). If the connection is established, you can exchange data with the counterpart over the connection (conversation).

UDP, however, is like sending a letter (via snail mail): you formulate a message, write the target address on the envelope, and throw the letter into a mail box. After that, you hope that the letter arrives, but this isn't certain – the address could be wrong or the letter could be simply lost on its way to the receiver. This is the case with UDP, too: you give a destination address for a data package and you just send it – but you won't get any notification whether the package ever arrived.

17.1 Sockets

Usually, you want to make sure that the data you are sending actually arrives, so TCP connections are preferred. In Java you have the "sockets" for creating TCP connections. With the help of sockets, you can create a connection between two endpoints. One of the endpoints is called the server, and the other is the client. The server is the one that waits for the client to establish a connection, whereas the client is the one who actually initiates the connection.

So in our analogy with the phone call, this would mean the one who gets called is the server. He is not actively involved in the process of establishing a connection, but he simply waits that he is called by someone else. The caller is the client: he establishes the connection by dialing the phone number.

Before we actually look at how this works, we must first know what should be used as an address for establishing TCP connections. With the phone call, this would be the phone number, but what's the address for network connections?

As you probably know, network connections are based on IP addresses. If a computer logs on to a network (e.g., when you connect to the Internet), the computer receives a unique number (the IP address) from the network, e.g., 217.12.28.255, so the computer can be addressed by this IP address later on. If we want to connect to a program running on a remote machine, the first thing we need is the IP address of the remote computer.

But the IP address alone is not enough. As you know, a computer can execute many programs at the same time. Imagine you create a connection to a machine with IP address 1.2.3.4. Your connection request arrives at the target machine and should be processed by the operating system. But how should the operating system know for which of its running programs the connection request is intended? (If we connect to a remote machine, we always want to connect to a specific program that processes the received data.)

So you can't establish a connection to a remote machine using its IP address only. You need some mechanism to indicate the specific program on the remote machine you want to connect to. You can do this using "ports."

A port is simply an (integer) number in the range from 1 to 65535. A server application can reserve a port and wait at this port until an incoming connection is received. You can imagine this as a harbor with different docks. The harbor represents the entire server machine. The individual programs are waiting at different docks (the ports) for arriving ships (i.e., incoming connections). So if we want to connect to a program on a remote machine, we need to know at which port the program is waiting in addition to the IP address.

If we create a server application on our own, we can freely select the port at which we want to wait for ingoing connections. Attention: there should be only one program waiting at every individual port; otherwise, there will be a conflict. The "lower" ports are blocked by basic Windows services already (see here [5] for a list of services); if we create a custom application, we should select a large port number to prevent a conflict with other applications. If you chose a port between 50,000 and 65,000, the probability is relatively low that there will be a collision with a different application. So these ports are best-suited for your own programs.

---

[5] https://en.wikipedia.org/wiki/List_of_TCP_and_UDP_port_numbers

17.1.1 Port Forwarding

We need to make another remark regarding the concept of the ports. It is rare nowadays that a computer is connected to the Internet directly. In most cases, a router is connected to the internet, so you can use multiple computers with a single line.

This introduces a new problem: the router receives a global IP address and all computers connected to the router use the same IP address when accessing the Internet. The problem is if you try to connect (from the outside) to a computer that is behind a router, the connection request doesn't arrive at that computer directly; instead, it arrives at the router. So the router receives a connection request that is actually intended for a machine that is connected to the router. But the router doesn't know the intended target machine, so it can't handle the connection request. The connection request is therefore discarded by the router.

So, it isn't normally possible to connect to a machine sitting behind a router. To make this possible, you need to make an adjustment to the router's port forwarding settings. For a router, you can specify that if there's a connection request on port XYZ, the request should be forwarded to computer ABC. Once you've made this setting, the router knows the intended target machine if a connection request arrives at a specific port. So it's possible to establish a connection from the outside.

For you, this means whenever you want to use a server application on a normal home computer operating behind a router, you need to forward the chosen server port to your target machine using your router's settings menu.

17.2 Server

So far in this chapter, we've looked at quite a lot of theory. Now we will see how to realize network functionality in Java, starting with a simple server application that waits for incoming connections:

```java
ServerSocket serverSocket = new ServerSocket(50000);

Socket clientConnection = serverSocket.accept();

InputStream is = clientConnection.getInputStream();
OutputStream os = clientConnection.getOutputStream();

int number1 = is.read();
int number2 = is.read();

int result = number1 + number2;

os.write(result);
os.flush();

clientConnection.close();
```

We create a server socket that listens for incoming connections on port 50,000. The class `ServerSocket` can be used to do this in Java. Using this class, you can wait for incoming connections. The wait operation is started by calling the method `accept()`: this method is "blocking" until an actual connection request arrives at the specified port. So if we call `accept()` and the first connection request arrives half an hour later, the program stands still for half an hour.

When a connection request is received, the method `accept()` automatically establishes the connection. The method returns an ordinary socket, which is a normal endpoint of a connection. To express this in the terms of our analogy with the telephone call, the socket is like the telephone receiver/handset. We can talk into the handset and we can listen to what the other side says. It's the same with the socket: we can write data into it (that will arrive at the other endpoint), and we can read data that has been written into the socket at the other endpoint.

In Java, there are the "streams" for reading and writing data from/to sockets. An input stream is a stream from which you can read data; and you can write data into an output stream.

The socket has both input and output streams. On the input stream, the data that has been written into the socket on the remote machine arrives. We can write data to the output stream ourselves, and this data will arrive in the input stream of the remote machine.

You can access the streams of a socket using the methods `getInputStream` and `getOutputStream`.

In our example, we use the input stream first. By calling the method `read()`, a single byte is read from the stream and returned as an `int` value. The method `read()` is blocking too: you can read from a stream only if the remote machine has already written some data into its output stream. So the `read()` method waits until there is data it can actually read.

So we read two bytes from the input stream. After that, we add the two numbers we obtained. We then use the output stream for sending the result of the addition back to the sender. The method `write()` of `OutputStream` sends a single byte to the remote machine.

Finally, we call the method `flush()` on the output stream, which enforces the actual sending of the data. But why do we need to do this? Well, it might be possible that the stream object decides internally it won't send the data directly, but instead waits until it has enough data and then sends all the data at once. We can prevent this by calling `flush()`, which will immediately dispatch all pending data.

So we've received two bytes via the network connection, performed an addition with these two bytes, and sent the result back to the sender. Finally, we can now disconnect the network connection by calling the method `close()` on the socket.

17.3 Client

Now we will have a look at the client application corresponding to the server shown above. So the client send two bytes via network to the server. After that, it should receive a value containing the sum of the two initial values back from the server.

The Java code is as follows:

```java
Socket socket = new Socket("localhost", 50000);

OutputStream os = socket.getOutputStream();
InputStream is = socket.getInputStream();

os.write(5);
os.write(12);
os.flush();

int result = is.read();

socket.close();

System.out.println("The result of the addition" +
            " received from the server is " + result);
```

Here you can see the constructor of the `Socket` class: you pass the IP address of the server as well as the desired port to the constructor, which will automatically establish the connection.

In our case, we didn't specify an IP address but used the term "localhost." This term means we don't want to connect to a remote machine, but to a different port on our own computer. This is a way to connect two programs running on the same machine. We could also have specified an IP address of a remote machine that is running our server application.

After the connection is established with the help of the socket, we use the methods `getOutputStream` and `getInputStream` for accessing the streams we use for data exchange. We write the values 5 and 12 into the output stream, and by calling `flush()`, we ensure the data is actually transferred to the remote machine. Now we listen on the input stream for the result that is to be delivered from the remote machine. The result should be the sum of the input values (i.e., 5 + 12 = 17). We store the result in the variable *result* and print the value on the console. Because the work is done, we also close the network connection by calling `close()` on the socket object.

In most cases, you wouldn't use these streams directly. There are more complex streams you can use for transferring complex objects over a network connection. However, we want use this simple example to demonstrate the basic principle of data transferring.

17.4 Access to Internet Resources

Using the previously introduced mechanism of the sockets, we could access all services that are implemented via TCP. This applies to web servers, for example: using socket programming, we can read Internet pages and process the data in our programs.

However, accessing Internet resources is a very common application of network technology within Java programs. So there are classes in Java that simplify web page access.

Let's start with the class URL: an instance of the class URL represents a simple Internet address:

```
URL myUrl = new URL("http://www.javaforbeginners.net");
```

The example shows a URL object that holds the Internet address of this book's website. But the address alone doesn't help much; we want to access the data that is stored at this address.

The class URL has a method openConnection() for establishing a connection to the appropriate web server.

```
URLConnection con = myUrl.openConnection();
```

We get an object of type URLConnection when calling openConnection(). This object corresponds approximately to the socket we know from simple TCP connections. We can access the input stream from this connection object and read the contents of the URL:

```
InputStream is = con.getInputStream();

StringBuffer sb = new StringBuffer();

int ch;
while ((ch = is.read()) != -1)
{
        sb.append((char) ch);
}

System.out.println(sb.toString());
```

This example introduces a couple of new concepts. First of all, we obtain the input stream from the connection object. Next, we create a StringBuffer object. A StringBuffer is similar to a string, except that a StringBuffer is mutable: we can add characters to the StringBuffer multiple times. Because we are going to read the input stream character by character, this is useful because it allows us to incrementally store the contents of the URL into a string.

The "while loop" seems interesting, too. A "while loop" will be executed as long as the condition of the loop is satisfied. But the condition in the example looks a little bit complicated, right? Let's take a closer look at it.

The condition of the loop is the following: `(ch = is.read()) != -1`

To the left we have the expression `ch = is.read()` enclosed in parentheses. This expression is a simple assignment, i.e., the previously created variable *ch* is assigned to the value that is read from the stream. After this assignment is completed, the condition is checked: `ch != -1`.

So we see how an assignment and a condition have been combined into a single instruction. The assignment (enclosed in parentheses) is executed first, and the result of the assignment is used for the comparison afterwards.

So the overall execution of the loop is as follows: a value is read from the stream. If the value is not -1, the body of the loop is executed; if the value read from the stream is -1, the loop will be terminated. So we read values from the stream until the end of the stream is reached; we have reached the end if the value that is read from the stream is -1.

We still have to analyze the body of the loop: `sb.append((char) ch);`

So the method `append()` is called on the `StringBuffer` object. Using this method, you can add characters to a `StringBuffer` (as the name already indicates). We've read a single value from the stream. The value is represented as an `int` number (i.e., by the ASCII code). To obtain the corresponding character, we perform an explicit type cast to the data type `char`.

Overall, the loop does the following: the input stream holding the contents of the Internet resource is read character by character. Because the characters that arrive are encoded with the ASCII code, we cast them directly into the data type `char`, so we can append them to the overall string (buffer). This way we read the overall content of the web resource incrementally and store it in a `StringBuffer` object.

At the end we can convert the `StringBuffer` object into an ordinary string using the method `toString()`. When printing the resulting string to the console, we should see the complete source code of the specified Internet address.

18 Graphical User Interfaces (GUIs)

For the conclusion of this Java book, we want to speak briefly about GUI programming. So far we've only seen very simple console applications: you start these programs, they generate a couple of outputs, and then they terminate. Console applications are well suited to demonstrate capabilities of Java. Developers often create "real" programs that run via the console. Such programs are controlled either via configuration files or via command line parameters.

In general, if you create a program that is intended for use by other people, you probably want to integrate a graphical user interface (GUI) into the program. The execution of a GUI application differs from the execution of a console application. In a console application, all instructions are executed one by one and the application automatically terminates afterwards. A GUI application, however, opens one or multiples windows and waits for user interaction. Depending on the user interaction, calculations and actions may be performed. In most cases, the application is terminated only upon user request, i.e., by clicking the close button at the top right of the title bar.

So if you develop a program with a GUI, the work flow is usually as follows: you create a user interface first, using some Java commands we will introduce shortly. The user interface should contain elements that allow for user interaction, such as buttons or input fields. After that, you can specify for every element that allows for interaction which task is to be executed upon interaction. So you can specify arbitrary code that is to be executed if a user interacts with a specific part of the GUI.

GUIs are usually realized using the "Swing" library. Older applications also use the "Abstract Window Toolkit" (AWT); however, this is considered out of date. So we will only look at the "Swing" user interfaces.

In this tutorial, we will introduce a very simple user interface only. There are various possibilities in Java for creating complex GUIs, but we will only demonstrate the basic principle here.

If we want to create an application with a GUI, we need a window that will contain the user interface. In Java there is the the class `JFrame`; an instance of this class represents a window.

18.1 A Minimalistic GUI

Let's first create a very simple minimalist application that only opens a window:

```java
public class MyFirstGui
{
    public static void main(String[] args)
    {
```

```
            JFrame f = new JFrame();

            f.setDefaultCloseOperation(JFrame.EXIT_ON_CLOSE);

            f.setVisible(true);
        }
}
```

For the sake of simplicity, we implement the entire program within the `main()` method. The program consists of only three instructions. First, a `JFrame` object is created; it will be the window of the application. On this object, we call the method `setDefaultCloseOperation()`. Using this method, you can specify what should happen if you click on the close button in the upper right corner of the title bar. There are various possibilities:

1. Nothing happens.

2. The windows disappears, but the program remains running in the background.

3. The program is terminated.

In most cases, you will select the third option: if the close button is clicked, you want the program to terminate. So we pass the statically declared constant `EXIT_ON_CLOSE` (i.e., it is a static attribute of class `JFrame`) to the method `setDefaultCloseOperation()`.

Using the third instruction `setVisible()`, we make the window visible now. So if a window is generated, it is not visible automatically; we have to make it visible explicitly. We can also make the window invisible again later by using `false` as the parameter for the call of `setVisible()`.

We can execute this simple program already. The program does exactly what you would expect: it opens a simple window without any content. The program isn't terminated directly after the three instructions of the program are executed, like a console application would be. Instead, the program runs until we close the windows using the close button.

18.2 GUI Elements

We would now like to create a GUI application with a window that has some content. To do so, it is a good idea to create a new class that is derived from the class `JFrame`. So we basically create an own window class that has properties and components that we specify.

Our own example window should consist of three elements: an input field, a button, and a result field. The user should be able to write a number into the input field, click the button and see the doubled number printed in the result field.

```java
public class GuiTest extends JFrame
{
        private JTextField textField = null;
        private JButton startButton = null;
        private JLabel resultLabel = null;

        public GuiTest() {
                setTitle("Calculating Doubles");

                setLayout(new FlowLayout());

                add(getTextField());
                add(getButton());
                add(getResultLabel());

                pack();

                setDefaultCloseOperation(EXIT_ON_CLOSE);
                setVisible(true);
        }

        private JLabel getResultLabel() {
                if (resultLabel == null) {
                        resultLabel = new JLabel();
                        resultLabel.setPreferredSize(
                                        new Dimension(250, 22));
                }
                return resultLabel;
        }

        private JTextField getTextField() {
                if (textField == null) {
                        textField = new JTextField();
                        textField.setPreferredSize(new Dimension(80, 22));
                }
                return textField;
        }

        private JButton getButton() {
                if (startButton == null) {
                        startButton = new JButton("Double it!");
                }
                return startButton;
        }

        public static void main( String[] args )
        {
                GuiTest gui = new GuiTest();
        }
}
```

So we create a subclass of `JFrame` for implementing our own window. The class has three private attributes: `textField`, `startButton`, and `resultLabel`.

The attribute `textField` is of type `JTextField`. `JTextField` objects are used to realize input fields in GUIs. The attribute `startButton` is of type `JButton`: this class implements buttons that enable clicking on them. Finally, we have the attribute `resultLabel` of type `JLabel`. `JLabel` objects implement simple labels (i.e., text in most cases) within a GUI.

Note: Until now, we only declared the corresponding attributes, but we haven't created the objects, and they aren't shown in our window yet. For creating these objects, we have created three methods: `getResultLabel()`, `getTextField()` and `getButton()`. These methods are quite simple: in every case, the constructor is called and an object of the respective type is created and stored within the correct variable (attribute). When calling the `JButton` constructor, we pass a `String` parameter, which specifies the label of the button. For the text field and the result label, we specify the optimal size for the objects when displayed within the window. We use a size of 80 x 22 pixels for the input field and a size of 250 x 22 pixels for the result label.

Our window is actually assembled in the constructor of the class. First of all, we specify a window title using `setTitle()` that is to be displayed in the title bar of the window. `setTitle()` is a method that was inherited from `JFrame`.

Next, we choose a layout for our window. There are various layouts in Java that allow for complex arrangement of the GUI elements. In this case, we are using the simplest layout: the `FlowLayout`. If you select a `FlowLayout` for a window, the elements that are added to the window are arranged one after the other, from left to right, from top to bottom.

The first component we add appears in the upper left corner of the window, the next component appears directly next, and so on, until the row is full. Additional components will then be added in the second row, from left to right, until the second row is full, and so on.

Once we have set this basic layout for our window, we can proceed to actually adding components to the window. The class `JFrame` has the method `add()` for doing so. Because we derived our class from the class `JFrame`, our window class `GuiTest` inherited the method `add()`, so the method `add()` can be used within the new class.

So we call the `add()` method three times to add our three components (input field, button, label) to the window. When calling `add()`, we pass the component that is to be added as a parameter to the method. Because we've written three methods that generate and return our components, we can use `getTextField()`, `getButton()`, and `getResultLabel()` as parameters when calling `add()`.

So we've added the three components to the window. We finally call the method `pack()`, which is inherited from the class `JFrame`. This method ensures the window and all of its components are the right size.

As we've already seen in the introductory example, we specify the behavior of the program when the close button is clicked (we want the program to terminate), and we make the window visible by calling `setVisible()`.

Now we can actually execute the program: we see a small window that contains the three components: an input field, a button, and a still-empty label. We can write numbers into the input field, and we can click on the button, but nothing happens when we do so.

But this shouldn't be a surprise; we didn't specify what should happen when the button is clicked. All we've done so far is construct the window and its components.

The desired behavior of the button is as follows: the number should be read from the input field, the double should be calculated, and the result should be displayed within the result label.

As a first step, we create a method within our class that performs the actions described above:

```java
private void calculateDouble()
{
        String numberAsString = getTextField().getText();
        int numberAsNumber = 0;
        String label = "";

        try {
                numberAsNumber = Integer.parseInt(numberAsString);
                numberAsNumber *= 2;

                label = "Doubled: " + numberAsNumber;
        } catch (NumberFormatException e) {
                label = "You specified an invalid number";
        }

        getResultLabel().setText(label);
}
```

The `JTextField` object (we access it using the method `getTextField()` implemented earlier) has a method `getText()`; we can read the text from the input field using this method. The text is always supplied as a string. After the call of `getText()`, we have a number that is stored in a string. To do calculations with this number, we have to convert it to a "number" data type. In this case, we use `int`.

We can perform the conversion with the help of the static method `parseInt()` of the `int` wrapper class `Integer`. This method attempts to convert a string to an `int` value. If this works, we store the value in an `int` variable and calculate the double value by multiplying it by 2. From the result we can generate the label that is intended to be shown to the user.

If the conversion from `String` to `int` doesn't work because there was no valid number in the input field, the method `parseInt` triggers a `NumberFormatException`. We catch this exception and generate a label that indicates the text input was not a valid number.

No matter whether the text can be converted to a number or not, we have a string object *label* that contains meaningful text: it's either the double of the input value or the note that the input specified was invalid.

Now we call the method `setText()` on the label object `resultLabel` (we access the label using the previously implemented method `getResultLabel()`). Using `setText()` we can change the text of the label. We pass the previously generated label as a parameter, so the label is now displayed in the `resultLabel`.

18.3 Event Handling

Until now, we've created a method containing some code we want to be executed as soon as the button is clicked. We now need to ensure that the method is actually executed when the user clicks the button.

In Java, there's the concept of event handlers for this. An event is a user interaction such as the click of a button or the insertion of text into an input field. A handler is a routine that is executed when a specific event occurs. You say you're registering an "event handler".

There are different types of event handlers. In our case, we need an `ActionListener`. To create our own custom `ActionListener`, we have to derive a new class from the base class `ActionListener`, and we need to override the method `actionPerformed()`. So we create a new class, and within the overridden method `actionPerformed()`, we specify what should happen if the handler is activated. Finally, we link the handler with the component it should monitor.

For the sake of clarity, we use inline technology to create an anonymous class again. We've seen this already when creating threads. Instead of creating a subclass of `ActionListener` within a new file, we derive it directly at the location where we want to use it and create a direct instance of it.

Overall, we extend the method `getButton()` as follows:

```java
private JButton getButton()
{
    if (startButton == null)
    {
        startButton = new JButton("Double it!");

        ActionListener actionListener = new ActionListener()
        {
            public void actionPerformed(ActionEvent e)
            {
                calculateDouble();
            }
        };
```

```
                startButton.addActionListener(actionListener);
        }
        return startButton;
}
```

We create a variable of type `ActionListener` with the name *actionListener*. We use the inline notation for definition and instantiation of an anonymous subclass of `ActionListener`. Within this class we override the method `actionPerformed()`. This method is called automatically from the system each time the button is clicked. The method has a parameter of type `ActionEvent`; it also has some additional information about the clicking. In our case we don't need that information; we just call the method `calculateDouble()` we created earlier. This method reads the number from the input field and writes the result of the computation to the result label.

So now that we have an `ActionListener` object, all that's left to do is to link it with the button so that the `ActionListener` is executed when the button is clicked. The class `JButton` has a method `addActionListener()` for doing so. We call this method on our button object and pass the object *actionListener* as a parameter. Now the button and the `ActionListener` are linked and the method `actionPerformed()` is executed each time the button is clicked. So our application now shows the desired behavior: if we enter a number and then click the button, the number is doubled and the result of this doubling is output.

19 Additional Web Resources

In the previous chapters, we introduced some of the most important concepts of the Java programming language. After you work through all chapters, you should be able to create your own simple Java programs. Furthermore, you should be able to understand simple code that other programmers have written.

But you should be clear about one thing: after reading this book, you are still not a professional programmer who can create large and complex applications. This is no surprise: you won't become a programmer overnight. Becoming a programmer is an ongoing process that requires learning and using more and more aspects of a programming language.

In this book, we have tried to cover as many as possible basic concepts of the Java programming language. Concepts are things such as data types, inheritance, and network programming. Each concept itself consists of countless aspects. You can think of an aspect of a programming concept as a subarea. When presenting a concept, we limited this to a part of the aspects. This tutorial is intended for Java (and programming) beginners, so we didn't want to flood the reader with too much information. Therefore, we presented the concepts in a way so you could get an overview over the concepts and gain a rough idea how they work.

This chapter will give you additional web resources that you can use to deepen your knowledge of Java. You will find additional information for most topics. It can be difficult for beginners to understand the countless instructions from the Internet. Once you've obtained an overview by working through this tutorial, you should be able to follow most of these web resources.

We've sorted the web pages according to the order we presented the topics within the tutorial. In some cases, we included hyperlinks to the official reference provided by "Oracle." A class reference specifies the purpose of a class and the exact functionality of all its methods. So the reference includes all methods of a class, and it includes explanations for all methods, so you know exactly what a method does.

Overall, there are more than fifty-five web pages listed in our resource index.

19.1 List of Web Resources

Java Application Programming Interface (API):
Official Documentation of all Java Classes (Oracle),
http://docs.oracle.com/javase/7/docs/api/

Eclipse:
Installation and Usage of Eclipse,
`https://www.csee.umbc.edu/courses/undergraduate/341/fall08/Lectures/Eclipse/intro-to-eclipse.pdf`

Java-Tools:
Basic Syntax of Java programs,
`https://www.tutorialspoint.com/java/java_basic_syntax.htm`

Bytecode:
Bytecode introduction,
`http://www.javaworld.com/article/2077233/core-java/bytecode-basics.html`

Variables:
Tutorial at jenkov.com,
`http://tutorials.jenkov.com/java/variables.html`
Tutorial at tutorialspoint.com,
`https://www.tutorialspoint.com/java/java_variable_types.htm`
Introduction at Wikibooks.org,
`https://en.wikibooks.org/wiki/Java_Programming/Variables`

if statement:
Introduction at Wikibooks.org,
`https://en.wikibooks.org/wiki/Java_Programming/Conditional_blocks`
Tutorial at Oracle.com,
`http://docs.oracle.com/javase/tutorial/java/nutsandbolts/if.html`
Tutorial at Tutorialspoint.com,
`http://www.tutorialspoint.com/java/java_decision_making.htm`

Loops:
Introduction at Wikibooks.org,
`https://en.wikibooks.org/wiki/Java_Programming/Loop_blocks`
Tutorial at Tutorialspoint.com,
`http://www.tutorialspoint.com/java/java_loop_control.htm`

switch statement:
Tutorial at Oracle.com,
`http://docs.oracle.com/javase/tutorial/java/nutsandbolts/switch.html`
Tutorial at Tutorialspoint.com,
`https://www.tutorialspoint.com/java/switch_statement_in_java.htm`

Overview at Dotnetperls.com,
`https://www.dotnetperls.com/switch-java`
Note: We didn't introduce the switch statement within this book. The switch statement is a construct that offers similar functionality like the if statement.

Object Orientation:
Introduction at Nanyang Technological University,
`https://www.ntu.edu.sg/home/ehchua/programming/java/J3a_OOPBasics.html`
Overview at Javaworld.com,
`http://www.javaworld.com/article/2979739/learn-java/java-101-classes-and-objects-in-java.html`
General Overview at Wikipedia.org,
`https://en.wikipedia.org/wiki/Object-oriented_programming`

Concepts of Object Orientation:
Überblick bei Oracle,
`http://docs.oracle.com/javase/tutorial/java/concepts/`
Tutorial bei Oracle,
`http://www.oracle.com/technetwork/java/oo-140949.html`

Primitive Data Types:
Wikibooks.org,
`https://en.wikibooks.org/wiki/Java_Programming/Primitive_Types`
Tutorial bei Oracle,
`http://docs.oracle.com/javase/tutorial/java/nutsandbolts/datatypes.html` (engl.)

Wrapper Classes:
Overview at W3Resource.com,
`http://www.w3resource.com/java-tutorial/java-wrapper-classes.php`

Type Casting:
Introduction at Blogsport.de,
`http://javarevisited.blogspot.de/2012/12/what-is-type-casting-in-java-class-interface-example.html`

Assignment and Operators:
Introduction at W3Resource.com,
`http://www.w3resource.com/java-tutorial/java-assignment-operators.php`

Summary at Oracle.com,
`https://docs.oracle.com/javase/tutorial/java/nutsandbolts/opsummary.html`
Tutorial at Wideskills.com,
`http://www.wideskills.com/java-tutorial/java-operators-tutorial`

Arrays:
Tutorial at Oracle.com,
`http://docs.oracle.com/javase/tutorial/java/nutsandbolts/arrays.html`
Introduction at Tutorialspoint.com,
`https://www.tutorialspoint.com/java/java_arrays.htm`
Two-dimensional Arrays,
`http://www.java67.com/2014/10/how-to-create-and-initialize-two-dimensional-array-java-example.html`
Multidimensional Arrays,
`http://www.homeandlearn.co.uk/java/multi-dimensional_arrays.html`

Reference of the Class Arrays:
Official Documentation at Oracle.com,
`http://docs.oracle.com/javase/7/docs/api/java/util/Arrays.html`
The Arrays class is a helping class for performing several operations on Array, for example, sorting or searching for elements.

Reference of the Class String:
Official Documentation at Oracle.com,
`http://docs.oracle.com/javase/7/docs/api/java/lang/String.html`

Strings:
Tutorial at Tutorialspoint.com,
`http://www.tutorialspoint.com/java/java_strings.htm` (engl.)
Tutorial at Oracle.com,
`https://docs.oracle.com/javase/tutorial/java/data/strings.html`

Classes:
Introduction at Wideskills.com,
`http://www.wideskills.com/java-tutorial/java-classes-and-objects`

References and Parameters:
Overview at Oracle.com,
`https://docs.oracle.com/javase/tutorial/java/javaOO/arguments.html`

Inheritance:
Introduction at Tutorialspoint.com,
`https://www.tutorialspoint.com/java/java_inheritance.htm`
Introduction at Javaworld.com,
`http://www.javaworld.com/article/2987426/core-java/java-101-inheritance-in-java-part-1.html`
Tutorial at Beginnersbook.com,
`http://beginnersbook.com/2013/03/inheritance-in-java/`

Exceptions:
Official Documentation at Oracle.com,
`http://docs.oracle.com/javase/tutorial/essential/exceptions/`
Tutorial at Wikibooks.org,
`https://en.wikibooks.org/wiki/Java_Programming/Throwing_and_Catching_Exceptions`

Generics Reference:
Tutorial at Oracle.com,
`http://docs.oracle.com/javase/tutorial/java/generics/`

Generics:
Introduction at Wikibooks.org,
`https://en.wikibooks.org/wiki/Java_Programming/Generics`
Introduction at Tutorialspoint.com,
`https://www.tutorialspoint.com/java/java_generics.htm`
Tutorial at javacodegeeks.com,
`http://www.javacodegeeks.com/2011/04/java-generics-quick-tutorial.html`

Collections:
Tutorial at Oracle.com,
`http://docs.oracle.com/javase/tutorial/collections/`
Tutorial at Javatpoint.com,
`http://www.javatpoint.com/collections-in-java`

Reference of the Collection Interfaces:
Offizielle Doku bei Oracle,
`http://docs.oracle.com/javase/7/docs/api/java/util/Collection.html`

Files:
Overview at Caveofprogramming.com,

https://www.caveofprogramming.com/java/java-file-reading-and-writing-files-in-java.html
Overview at Wikibooks.org,
https://en.wikibooks.org/wiki/Java_Programming/Streams

DataStreams:
Short Introduction,
http://www.codingeek.com/java/io/data-streams-a-convinient-read-write-primitives-in-java/

Object Streams:
Tutorial at Codingeek.com,
http://www.codingeek.com/java/io/object-streams-serialization-deserialization-java-example-serializable-interface/

Concurrency:
Concepts of Concurrency,
http://tutorials.jenkov.com/java-concurrency/index.html
Introduction at Winterbe.com,
http://winterbe.com/posts/2015/04/07/java8-concurrency-tutorial-thread-executor-examples/
Tutorial at Oracle.com,
http://docs.oracle.com/javase/tutorial/essential/concurrency/
Tutorial at vogella.com,
http://www.vogella.com/articles/JavaConcurrency/article.html

Reference of Class Thread:
Official Documentation at Oracle.com,
http://docs.oracle.com/javase/7/docs/api/java/lang/Thread.html

Network Programming:
Socket Overview at Oracle.com,
http://docs.oracle.com/javase/tutorial/networking/sockets/
Tutorial at Javaworld.com,
http://www.javaworld.com/article/2077322/core-java/core-java-sockets-programming-in-java-a-tutorial.html
HttpURLConnection Example,
https://www.mkyong.com/java/how-to-send-http-request-getpost-in-java/

Reference of the Package java.net:

Official Documentation at Oracle.com,
http://docs.oracle.com/javase/7/docs/api/java/net/package-summary.html

GUI-Programmierung:
Overview at New York University,
http://cs.nyu.edu/~yap/classes/visual/03s/lect/17/
Introduction at Codeproject.com,
http://www.codeproject.com/Articles/33536/An-Introduction-to-Java-GUI-Programming
Tutorial at Zetcode.com,
http://zetcode.com/tutorials/javaswingtutorial/

Swing Reference:
Official Documentation at Oracle.com,
http://docs.oracle.com/javase/7/docs/api/javax/swing/package-summary.html

20 Example Code Downloads

Here you can download the Java source code of the programming examples from all chapters in this book. You can import the code directly into your development environment and execute it.

You should play around with the code. Feel free to alter the code and observe how the execution (and output) changes. This way you can develop a feeling for the code.

20.1 Download

Download of Java Code[6]

20.2 Import

To use the code within the "Eclipse" development environment, you should take the following steps.

1. Create a new project. (File → New → Java Project)

2. Choose a suitable name for the project, e.g., "JavaTutorial."

3. Make sure the option "Create separate folders for sources and class files" is activated at the "Project Layout" section.

4. Remember the physical address of the project that is given in the "Location" field.

5. Create the project by clicking "Finish."

6. Navigate to the directory where the project has been saved using Windows Explorer. Change to the subdirectory "src." Unzip the contents of the zip file to this directory.

7. In Eclipse, you should see the project with the name you've chosen in the package explorer at the left. Right-click on the name of the project ("JavaTutorial", if you followed our suggestion). From the context menu that should appear now, select the option "Refresh."

8. The code should be imported automatically. You can navigate through the "src" tree now; you will see the individual packages and classes. If you double click on a class, it will open in the editor window to the right.

---

[6]http://www.javaforbeginners.net/go/tutorialcode_en.zip

9. You can execute all classes that have a `main()` method. To do this, select the class you want to execute in the package explorer, so the corresponding file will open in the source editor. Open the context menu of the toolbar icon with the green-white arrow (i.e., click on the small, downward-pointing arrow next to the icon) and select Run As → Java Application.

20.3 Exercises

You will find the exercises and the sample solutions online on the book's website.[7]

21 Imprint

Lorig, Daniel: Java-Programming for Beginners: Learn Programming without Previous Knowledge
Nalbach, October 2016

All rights of this work are the exclusive property of the author:
Daniel Lorig
Schillerstr. 18
66809 Nalbach

Germany

ISBN-10: 153976446X
ISBN-13: 978-1539764465

---

[7] http://www.javaforbeginners.net/online-exercises/

Made in the USA
Lexington, KY
31 January 2018